THE OFFICIAL

JOEL EISNER

CONTEMPORARY
BOOKS, INC.
CHICAGO ▪ NEW YORK

Library of Congress Cataloging-in-Publication Data

Eisner, Joel, 1959–
  The official Batman batbook.

    1. Batman (Television program)   I. Title.
PN1992.77.B343E57   1986   791.45′72   86-4517
ISBN 0-8092-5035-7 (pbk.)

Published by Contemporary Books, Inc.
180 North Michigan Avenue, Chicago, Illinois 60601
Manufactured in the United States of America
Library of Congress Catalog Card Number: 86-4517
International Standard Book Number: 0-8092-5035-7

Published simultaneously in Canada by Beaverbooks, Ltd.
195 Allstate Parkway, Valleywood Business Park
Markham, Ontario L3R 4T8 Canada

CONTENTS

This book is dedicated to all of the arch villains of
Gotham City, without whom Batman would be out of work.

ACKNOWLEDGMENTS

I would like to thank the following people for their help in making this book a reality:

Tom Emma of ABC Video Enterprises

Judy Fireman of DC Comics

Sandra L. Gottlieb of 20th Century-Fox

Also: Hermione Baddeley, Richard Bakalyan, Anne Baxter, Robert Butler, Roger C. Carmel, Yvonne Craig, William Dozier, Charles FitzSimons, Alan Hale, Jr., Barrie Howard, Leslie H. Martinson, Diane McBain, Roddy McDowall, Burgess Meredith, Lee Meriwether, Robert Mintz, Alan Napier, Julie Newmar, Michael Pate, Vincent Price, Cliff Robertson, Cesar Romero, Stanley Ralph Ross, Howard Schwartz, Ellis St. Joseph, Joey Tata, Malachi Throne, Rik Vollaerts, Eli Wallach.

Plus: Allan Asherman, Patrick Culliton, Joe Desris, Irving Fuentes, Joe Hill, Jerry Ohlinger, Patrick White, and Michael Woodin.

James H. Burns (for the Burgess Meredith interview, portions of which previously appeared in Rod Serling's *Twilight Zone* magazine).

David Krinsky (for the Yvonne Craig interview).

Special thanks go to Jody Rein, of Contemporary Books, and Neal Matte.

INTROD

On Wednesday January 12, 1966, the world of television was changed forever. On that night at 7:30 P.M. (EST) Batman made his prime time debut.

The series was unlike anything else that had ever appeared on prime time television. It was to create one of the biggest "fads" this country would ever know and till this very day the country still wonders, "why?" Many people wonder why a series based on a comic book could have become such an overnight success, while previous attempts at comic book based shows such as Superman and Dick Tracy never did.

The answer to this question is both an easy and a difficult one. On the surface, the Batman series, unlike previous efforts, was constructed so that it appealed to the television audience on two levels. It appealed to the youth of America in that it was a living comic book. It had the action and adventure that the kids just loved. At the same time, it also appealed to the adult audience with its camp humor and well-known celebrities. This was a rare program that parents and children could watch together and enjoy simultaneously.

So much for the easy answer. But who's to say what makes a cult a cult? Something that grabs something indefinable for thousands of people, something that makes people so identify with a phenomena that he or she wants to be a part of it, to belong to it, through wearing T-shirts, flaunting merchandise, collecting memorobilia. "Batman" tapped that desire.

I first encountered Batman when I was six years old. I had been reading the comic books, so I was no stranger to the caped crusader. It did take a number of viewings to get used to the fast-paced show, but when I did, I was hooked.

Years later I learned to appreciate the series on a different level, that which the adult population at the time of the series enjoyed—the wonderful campy performances of the villains, the outrageous and wild situations which occurred on the show. After seeing several books appearing across the country praising the accomplishments of other television series and waiting in vain for a book on Batman to appear, I decided that I would take matters in hand and write the book myself.

As a fan of the show as well as a writer, I have endeavored to find as many of the people as I could who had worked and/or appeared on the series in order to obtain their insights, feelings, and stories about the Batman series. In doing this I have tried to recapture the flavor of the series and have eliminated the usual misinformation and conjecture which I've sometimes found in other television-oriented books.

Besides the above-mentioned items, I have included a detailed episode guide to the entire series and the feature film including complete sets of credits. A comprehensive checklist of every HOLY word uttered by Robin, a complete checklist to all of the BatEquipment, a complete checklist to every BatFight word and even a BatTrivia quiz. Plus a collection of photographs, the majority of which have never before appeared in print.

While I found most people I interviewed to be receptive and helpful in putting this book together, there were, of course some who declined to be interviewed or for various reasons were unavailable when this book was being put together. I would like to state for the record that regardless of their inclusion herein, they shall remain a part of the Batman legacy which will endure long after they have departed for that great big belfrey in the sky.

If you have any comments, questions, criticisms, or additional information please feel free to write to me in care of the publisher.

So, without further ado . . . TO THE BATMOBILE!

As the Bat Turns

The character of Batman was created by Bob Kane and made his first appearance in *Detective Comics #27*, in 1939. Despite his popularity, he did not make his first film appearance until 1943, when Columbia Pictures turned the Caped Crusader into a movie serial entitled, simply, *Batman*. It starred two relative unknown actors named Lewis Wilson and Douglas Croft as Batman and Robin. Any resemblance between the characters as they appeared in the comic books and as they were portrayed in the movie serial was purely coincidental. The only other character besides the Dynamic Duo that made the transition to the serial was Alfred the butler. For some unexplained reason, Batman was also given a girlfriend named Linda in the movies. The only saving grace in the serial was the villainous Dr. Daka, played by the wonderful charater actor J. Carroll Nash.

Five years later, Columbia decided to take another chance on Batman by releasing another serial, entitled *Batman & Robin*. Columbia replaced the former Dynamic Duo with actors Robert Lowery and John Duncan. Alfred was nowhere to be seen; however, Lyle Talbot showed up as Commissioner Gordon. The duo fought a villain called the Wizard, but once again the serial left much to be desired. It was not until 1966, when the "Batman" TV series was created, that the comic book hero was transferred successfully to film.

The popularity of the "Batman" TV series laid the foundation for other TV manifestations of Batman and his cohorts.

During the late 1960s, an animated version of "Batman" turned up on Saturday morning television. These cartoons were very successful and ran for several years. Then, in 1977, another animated verson of "Batman" was done, and this time the cartoons used the voices of Adam West and Burt Ward, reprising their Batman and Robin roles. A couple of years later, two live-action specials were made in the hope of reviving the "Batman" series. West and Ward re-

turned, along with Frank Gorshin as the Riddler, but they were only a small part of the shows which also included several other heroes and villains. The specials were cheaply done on videotape, and it showed. Adam West has since gone on to play the voice of Batman in the "Super Friends" cartoon series. But, regardless of how many more versions turn up in the years to come, the original television series is and always will be the best version.

The fact is borne out not only by fans' continuing interest in the now-defunct show, but also by the enthusiasm with which cast and production staff members recall their "Batman" experiences. On the following pages, several "Batman" insiders give us a closer look at how the series evolved.

William Dozier, who became executive producer of the show, started his career as a literary agent before becoming the head of the writing and story department at Paramount Studios. Six years later, Dozier moved over to RKO where he became the executive assistant to Charles Koerner, then head of production.

In 1951, he joined CBS as their executive producer of dramatic programs and was later promoted to the position of vice president in charge of Hollywood programming.

In 1959, Dozier moved to Columbia Pictures as the vice president in charge of their television division, Screen Gems.

In 1964, he left Screen Gems to form his own production company, Greenway Productions.

Dozier relates how he got involved in the birth of "Batman."

"I had never read a *Batman* comic book; I had never read *any* comic book. When I was growing up, I read *David Copperfield*, *Great Expectations*, and the things you are supposed to read. Doug Cramer was then assistant to Edgar Sherick, who was then head of programming for ABC in New York. Both of them were stationed in New York. A fellow named Harve Bennett, who later produced the *Star Trek* movies, was their top man out here in Los Angeles, but he didn't have much authority. All of the decisions were made in New York at ABC. Cramer called and asked me if I would be interested in producing 'Batman,' saying they had acquired the rights. I said, 'Well, let me think about it,' which is a sophist's way of saying, 'I don't know anything about it, but I will find out.'

"How they happened to acquire the rights is very interesting. They were naturally looking for ways to strengthen their programming. So, a guy in the lower echelon in the programming department, whose name I did know at the time but have long since forgotten [Mr. Benvegna], was not one of the two or three top guys (he was down the ladder), but he suggested that they look into the area of comic books as possible source material for seven-thirty programming, which was then prime time. They had a research outfit question people in supermarkets, churches, schools, and so on, about which shows they would rather see on television. They had Superman, Dick Tracy, Batman, Green Hornet, and Little Orphan Annie. Superman was the number one choice, Dick Tracy was the number two choice, Batman three, Green Hornet four, and Little Orphan Annie five. They couldn't get the rights to Superman, not because of the old George Reeves series, because their rights had long since evaporated, but because there was a Broadway show called *It's a Bird, It's a Plane, It's Superman*, and that is what stopped them. They couldn't get Dick Tracy, because Chester Gould was in some

kind of peripheral negotiations with NBC, which never came to anything. (As a matter of fact, later, after 'Batman' went on, everybody wanted to do the same kind of show. I made a deal with Chester Gould to do the pilot for 'Dick Tracy.' I didn't think it was very good. I had very little stomach for trying to copy 'Batman.' I did try not to copy it, but I tried to duplicate it with 'Green Hornet.' How are you going to be serious about a guy who runs a newspaper in the daytime and goes out at night and hunts criminals? How can you be funny with it? It just fell in the middle. It was neither serious nor funny.)

"Anyway, I told them, 'I am coming to New York next week. I will talk to you about it then.' I had never worked with Cramer, but we knew each other. I went to New York, and after the meeting I scurried around and bought maybe seven or eight different vintage copies of the *Batman* comic books. I got on a plane coming back, and I was sitting there in an aisle seat, with these things in my lap, as I didn't have time to read them in New York. I remember Bud Barry, who was the head of television for Young and Rubicam, the ad agency at the time, came up the aisle, looked over my shoulder, saw me reading these comics, and said, 'I guess those scripts do get a little dull after a while.' Now, I couldn't tell him why a full-grown man was sitting there with a lap full of *Batman* comic books, because it was a big secret. I felt a little bit like an idiot. Then I digested all of those books. At first, I thought they were crazy. I really thought they were crazy, if they were going to try to put this on television. Then I had just the simple idea of overdoing it, of making it so square and so serious that adults would find it amusing. I knew kids would go for the derring-do, the adventure, but the trick would be to find adults who would either watch it with their kids or, to hell with the kids, and watch it anyway.

"I called Cramer and told him, 'I will be back in New York next week. I will come and talk to you about it.' So, he had the whole ABC organization lined up in a room around this huge table. Leonard Goldenson, Tom Moore, who was head of the television operations at that time, Sherrick, two or three other people, and I tell them the story of Batman, whose mother and father were killed by dastardly criminals, and he took an oath for the rest of his life that he would avenge their deaths. They looked at me, and they thought I was a little crazy. I said, 'That, gentlemen, is his motivation, and he dedicates his life to fighting crime.' Then I explained how we were going to do it—that we were going to have 'ZAP' and 'POW.' And I remember Leonard Goldenson said, 'We are going to have, right on the screen, "ZAP" and "POW"?' I said, 'Yeah, and a lot more, Leonard.' 'Oh, my,' he said.

"I made a deal with them, and they said, 'OK, you go ahead and do whatever you want to do.' So, I got Lorenzo Semple, whom I knew well (and I knew that he had a short-circuited mind). He was in Spain, working on something else. So, I flew to Madrid, and he drove up to meet me, and we sat in the garden of the Ritz Hotel, where I was staying. While drinking three bottles of Spanish wine, and having lunch, we hatched out the whole plot for the pilot film. Then he wrote it, and I produced it and cast it. I had no problem from ABC about any of the casting; they didn't question anything.

"When we had the pilot film finished, we took it to the preview theater outfit, where people sit with little dials, which they turn one way when they are enjoying it and the other way when they are not enjoying it. A guy named Pierre Marquis ran that thing, and I think he still does. I used to call it 'Pierre Marquis and His Puppets,' because it seemed stupid to me. By the time people see something and react to it, they have forgotten, and they turn it later, so the registration comes up about nine beats too late. But they never bothered to figure that out.

"They had the lowest rating that night of anything they had ever tested at the preview theater! Fortunately, it was no longer a pilot test, because ABC was so desperate for something to put on at seven-thirty to try to capture the audience early (which is the trick of television), that on the basis of the little bit of footage they had seen earlier, they 'already ordered it up,' as they used to say. They ordered thirteen episodes. I remember that Sherrick and Cramer were out here that night we tested that thing, and we went to the Beachcomber for dinner afterward, and it was a funeral procession. Because it was *their* money, they all figured (except me, I did not think so) we had the biggest disaster in the world on our hands, and we had already bought it. I remember driving home that night, and I said to my wife, Ann Rutherford, who used to be an actress, 'You know, if that goddamn machine is right and I am wrong about this, I am going to get out of the business. There is no place for me if I can be that wrong.' Well, the rest is history."

Charles FitzSimons, who served as assistant to the executive producer also remembers the ironically dismal preview ratings:

"When they tested the pilot at the preview theater, it got a rating of fifty-two. The passing grade was sixty-two. The network executives panicked. They had bought an entire run of episodes, and this was going to be the biggest bomb in history. So, they decided to see if there was anything they could do to salvage it. They came to us and asked if we would put a laughtrack on the film. We said OK, provided we could take it back to the theater for another test. They said OK, and we put the laughtrack on the film and took it to the theater. It got the same rating of fifty-two that it got without the laughtrack. They then asked us to put an introduction on the beginning of the show, informing the audience that this was a comedy and that the audience should hiss the villains and cheer for the heroes. They thought the audience didn't know what they were watching. We tried it, and again it didn't work. So, finally they left it alone, and when it finally aired it was a big success."

What *did* make "Batman" such a big success? There is no doubt that the show struck audiences as funny, but it certainly wasn't a standard sitcom. As William Dozier mentioned earlier, the humor in the series came from overdoing it in such a fashion that it

was so straight that it had to be funny. Dozier elaborates:

"I found out, a year later, that the network hadn't wanted a so-called *broad* comedic approach to the show. They had sense enough to know that you can't make it tumble-down slapstick, and I had a background of dramatic shows. I had been an executive producer of dramatic shows in New York for CBS and for CBS in Los Angeles, and was involved with 'Playhouse 90,' 'Climax,' and this was my whole background, never comedy. But that is what they wanted, so obviously it worked."

The producers of "Batman" obviously had hit on the right formula for comedic success with the series, but they couldn't have carried it off without the right actors. Producer Dozier recalls how the casting for the show was handled:

"My first choice for Batman was Ty Hardin, but he was shooting spaghetti westerns in Italy, so was unavailable. His agent came in to tell me that Ty couldn't try out, and then he showed me an eight-by-ten. He said, 'What do you think of this guy?' So this was a guy with a surfboard walking on the beach, who looked good. He had been in three or four episodes of 'Robert Taylor and the Detectives,' which I had never seen. So, I had never seen him. I said, 'Well, he looks good. Have him come in. If he understands what we are trying to do, we will make a test of him.' So , he came in, and I had a long talk with him. He's very bright, Adam, and when I explained to him that it had to be played as though we were dropping a bomb on Hiroshima, with that kind of deadly seriousness—that he wasn't going to be Cary Grant, full of charm, but just had to play a very square, hard-nosed guy—and I said, 'Hopefully, it is going to be funny.' He got it right away and understood what we were trying to sell.

"We made a test of him and Lyle Waggoner. The only reason we also tested Lyle Waggoner is because I knew from my experiences with the networks that you have to give them a choice. You can't just say, 'This

is the guy.' You say, 'Here are two guys. We like them both, but we like one much better than the other. We want you to see them both.' They say, 'Which one do you like better?' We said we liked Adam West better, then they would say, 'Oh, we do too.' But if you didn't give them another choice, they'd say, 'Can't you test someone else, too?' So, that's the way their heads work and always have, and I suppose mine worked that way, too, when I was a network exeuctive.

"I also had a prior choice for the police captain, but I couldn't get him, so I settled for Stafford Repp, who was very good.

"Everybody else, like Neil Hamilton, was no contest. I had known Neil for years, and I knew he was exactly right for the commissioner. Aunt Harriet was a character we made up. That was to keep them from looking like homosexuals. We put a woman in the house to balance the act. I remember Jules Feiffer, the cartoonist, gave out a couple of interviews when the show was first a hit, implying that there was a homosexual relationship between Bruce Wayne and Dick Grayson. So, I made a lot of appearances at that time, when the show was at its zenith, and peole would ask me about that. I said, 'If Jules Feiffer thinks that, he is just a dirty old man,' and that would end the whole discussion. No question, Yvonne Craig was the only choice for Batgirl, and Alan Napier for Alfred." [The character of Aunt Harriet originally appeared in the June 1964 issue of *Detective Comics*, nearly two years before the series pilot was ever made. Regardless of Dozier's recollection, the Aunt Harriet character did exist two years before the series.]

Actor **Alan Napier** who protrayed Alfred, Batman's faithful butler, began his career playing kings and prime ministers in his native England before making his American debut as a coal miner in the 1940 Vincent Price film *The Invisible Man Returns*. The role of Alfred was a new experience for Mr. Napier as it was the first time he had ever played a butler in his then forty-three year career (Alan was born on January 7, 1903). Alan recalls how he first became associated with the Batman series:

"I was actually the first person hired for "Batman," before Batman or Robin or anybody, because Charles FitzSimons was an associate of my agent years before and had moved on to be Dozier's assistant. He, for some reason, envisioned me as Alfred because, after all, what I did as Alfred was quite different from what was written. He sold the idea to Dozier, and I was hired. I have never read comics before I did it. My agent rang up and said, 'I think you are going to play on "Batman," ' I said, 'What is "Batman"?' He said, 'Don't you read the comics?' I said, 'No, never.' He said, 'I think you are going to be Batman's butler.' I said, 'How do I know I want to be Batman's butler?' It was the most ridiculous thing I had ever heard of. He said, 'It may be worth over $100,000.' So I said I was Batman's butler.

"It was very clever casting—the whole thing was. I didn't have much character guidance in the first episode. When I went to see Dozier about my moustache—I wanted to know if he wanted me to shave it off or not—I asked him about his ideas about the charcter. He said, 'I just want you to be yourself.' The character of Alfred has a last name of Pennyworth in the comics, but we never used it on the series."

As fans will remember, the narration was a big part of the overall flavor of the "Batman" series. The narrator had to express the same overserious tone as the actors. As William Dozier describes, the choice of narrator became as important as the rest of the casting.

"We auditioned several professional voice-over people, maybe seven or eight. I would go into the dubbing room, and the crew and the audition guy would be there. It just wasn't right. I would give them a sample of how I thought it should sound, and finally one of them said, 'Bill, there is only one person who should do this, and as much as I would like to have the job, *you* should do it.' Then I found out that the sound crew had been telling Charlie FitzSimons that all along. Charlie kept saying, 'Why doesn't he do it?'

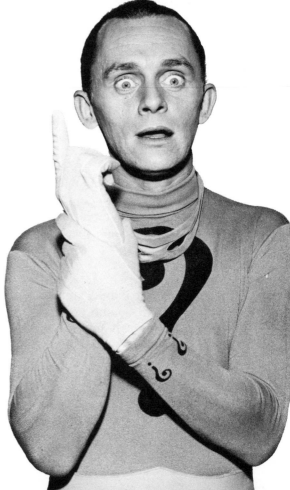

9

"So now we were down to the nitty-gritty: we needed a piece of film for the network to show advertisers. They had ordered the show, and they wanted to sell it. It had to be tied together with some kind of narration, so I said, 'OK, I'll do it for this film.' So, they all came out from New York to look at this piece of film, which was ten minutes long. When it was over, they had liked it. And Tom Moore said, 'That voice, that narrator—we got him signed up, haven't we?' I said, 'Oh, no, we can't touch him, Tom. He is a very busy fellow.' And I milked that for about five minutes and finally told him who it was. Then I had to join the Screen Actor's Guild in order to do it, and then I discovered that SAG has the best medical plan in the business, so when I finished with 'Batman,' and when the reruns had run their course— eight runs domestic and five runs foreign, I think—I did a lot of stuff around town and on various other shows, small parts, in order to keep the medical plan. Now that I am retired, I get the same benefits from the SAG, and don't have to work at all. So, it worked out very well."

As often happens with premiering TV series—especially when there has been significant doubt about the potential success of the show—early production of "Batman" was a hurry-up-and-wait situation. Director of photography **Howard Schwartz** recalls those hectic days:

"We had a problem on the show because when ABC bought it they didn't give the go-ahead on it until November, and they wanted to put the shows on in January. So, although usually you get three or four months lead time into a show, we didn't have this luxury, so we had to go to two units (two camera crews to shoot the film in half the time), and the editors and everyone were working Saturdays and Sundays, just continuously. It made it tough on everybody. You were always fighting time, and the hours were very long.

"The cameramen would always try to hurry these things up, and one of the problems was that sometimes Adam would come in late, and I used to get on his case a little bit. I guess I finally got to him, so he complained to Dozier. So, one day I was told by Sam Strangis, who was our production manager, to go see Dozier. So, I went and talked with Bill, and he got on me pretty good about this thing. You know, 'Adam's our star, and you shouldn't talk to him that way, and you should really let up on him.' I said OK, and as I started to walk out the door, he said, 'Howard, don't let up on him too much.' (Adam and I are good friends now, and I see him quite a bit.)"

Production is crucial to all TV programs, but was even more so to "Batman," whose special effects were unique to television at that time and were instrumental in drawing the show's enormous audience. These unusual techniques were not produced without problems, however, so postproduction coordinator Robert Mintz explains:

"The expenses for the opticals from this series were enormous. The "POW," "BAM," etc., were all to be done optically, by taking the original negative and making an interpositive of it. You then take the interpositive and do the artwork and the lettering, and you put the "POW" over the scene, and it takes a lot of time and costs a lot of money. [In other words, originally viewers would have seen the words at the same time as the fights—in the same frame.] The optical bills were coming in, and they were astronomical. So, they said to me, 'What can we do to reduce the cost of these opticals? Or are we going to have to eliminate most of them and do maybe one "POW" per show.' I said to myself, 'What if we made up a whole roll of these things? We make up the title against different color backgrounds and edit a few frames of them into the show. It is not an optical effect at all. The scene is all original. Then, when you do the fight, on the impact of the punch you cut in a few frames of the "POW," and then you come back to the fight. It worked; they loved it. We had three cutting rooms, and each cutting room had a roll of different colored fight words, and they would peel them off and edit them into the film."

Despite such innovations, "Batman" remained an expensive show to produce—so much so, in fact, that high expenses played a role in the series' eventual demise. William Dozier comments:

"The show became too expensive for the time period. It was a very expensive show to do because of all the special effects. It became too expensive for the number of people who were watching at that time—the right kind of people, the people who spend money on the sponsor's product. That's when they discovered the word *demographics*. Choirs would change their night for rehearsal. I remember going over to USC once for something, and all the dorms on Wednesday night were watching 'Batman.'

"I remember being in New York once during the show and going into 21, and if you turn sharply to the right there is sort of a lounge room with a big television set. I remember going in there one Wednesday or Thursday night and being absolutely astounded that there were maybe thirty people in there watching 'Batman.' In New York, a very sophisticated crowd went to 21 at that time. I never cease to be in awe of the way it grabbed everybody. Of course, that proved to be the trick of the show, making it amusing to adults. We did a lot of research then, and we discovered that kids became interested in it at about the age of four. At the age of about fifteen or sixteen, they lost interest, because they felt that they were too grown up for it. Then, when they got to be about eighteen or nineteen, they became interested in it again."

CAST & CREW*

BATMAN CREDITS

Batman/Bruce Wayne—Adam West
Robin/Dick Grayson—Burt Ward
Alfred—Alan Napier
Commissioner Gordon—Neil Hamilton
Chief O'Hara—Stafford Repp
Aunt Harriet Cooper—Madge Blake
Batgirl/Barbara Gordon—Yvonne Craig (third
    season only)
Warden Crichton—David Lewis (semi-regular)
Mayor Linseed—Byron Keith (semi-regular)
Executive Producer & Narrator—William
    Dozier
Producer—Howie Horwitz
Assistant to Executive Producer—Charles
    FitzSimons
Associate Producer—William P. D'Angelo
Script Editor—Charles Hoffman
Script Consultant—Lorenzo Semple, Jr.
Music—Nelson Riddle
Title Theme—Neal Hefti

* Cast regulars listed here; guest cast
members are listed for each episode.

Most Commonly Used
BatEquipment**

Batarang
Batphone
Batsignal
Batcycle
Batmobile
Batcopter
Batboat
Batshield
Batpoles
Batrope
Batcuffs
Batcostumes/Batsuit
Batsleep
Batawake
Utility Belt
Batcave

**Regularly used BatEquipment listed here; special equipment are listed for each episode.

First Season

1—HI DIDDLE RIDDLE
2—SMACK IN THE MIDDLE

GUEST CAST

Riddler—Frank Gorshin
Molly—Jill St. John
Inspector Basch—Michael Fox
Gideon Peale—Damian O'Flynn
Moldavian Prime Minister—Ben Astar
Newscaster—Jack Barry
Doorman—Dick Reeves
Maitre d'—William Dozier

Teleplay & story by Lorenzo Semple, Jr.
Directed by Robert Butler
Production #6028
Original air dates: 1/12/66 & 1/13/66

PLOT

Hi Diddle Riddle. Gotham City World's Fair is hardly the place where you would expect to find criminal activity. Or would you? Even now, at the pavilion of the Republic of Moldavia, the Riddler's scheme to use the law against Batman is beginning, as the Moldavian prime minister prepares to cut into the Moldavian Friendship cake.

Unknowingly, the prime minister sets off the hidden bomb inside the cake, releasing a concealed riddle. This riddle leads the Dynamic Duo to the Peale Art Gallery, where they are duped into arresting the "innocent" Riddler. Batman is sued for false arrest!

Batman must uncover the Riddler's plan before the case comes to trial, or he will be forced to reveal his true identity in court, ending his crime-fighting career forever.

Two cleverly hidden riddles in the legal documents lead Batman and Robin to the new discotheque, What a Way to Go-Go! There the Riddler's plan is once again put into action. Being a minor, Robin is legally unable to enter the disco, so he'll have to wait outside in the Batmobile while Batman enters alone.

While Batman dances the Batusi with the Riddler's assistant Molly, Robin falls victim to the Riddler's tranquilizer dart gun and is carried away down a manhole by the Riddler and his Molehill Mob. Batman, having drunk a glass of drugged orange juice, finds himself in no condition to pursue them.

Meanwhile, in the Riddler's hideout, Robin is being strapped down on a table as the Riddler prepares to operate on the unconscious boy!

Smack in the Middle. Riddler's Robin "operation" involved only the making of a plaster cast from Robin's masked face, used to make a perfect "Robin" mask for Molly.

After enticing Batman with riddles, the Riddler and Molly (dressed as Robin) lead Batman on a merry chase before their car is disabled by the Batray. The Riddler makes his escape as Molly tricks Batman into taking her to the Batcave.

At the Batcave, our keen-eyed hero spots the defect in the mask caused by the straws they gave Robin to breathe through. Batman chases the now unmasked, disarmed fleeing

16

girl to the top of the atomic pile (used to power the Batmobile), where she slips and falls to her dastardly death.

Batman rescues the real Robin, but that rambunctious Riddler manages to escape to the Moldavian Pavilion, where a gathering honors the famous Mammoth of Moldavia, which is stuffed with used, now priceless, Moldavian postage stamps. The Riddler, planning to steal the Mammoth, floods the pavilion with laughing gas. Then, dressed in an outrageous costume and elephant mask (which hides his gas mask), he entertains the crowd with a few jokes until everyone has passed out laughing. Riddler and his Mob blast a hole in the floor, and are about to escape when the Dynamic Duo save the day! Leaping out from inside the huge beast, they subdue the entire Mob. The Riddler retreats—and may or may not explode with a tank of laughing gas. Will he return? Tune in again—same Batbook, new Batpage. (The lawsuit, by the way, was dismissed, for the Riddler was a no-show.)

BatTalk
Director Robert Butler

"I remember, when I first got on it, Lorenzo Semple (story writer) and I were kind of social friends, and he came over and started talking about this thing. It sounded really nuts, and it was. Even the crew was confused at first. When, after Molly (Jill St. John) falls into the power core, Batman (Adam West) first leaned over the rail and said, 'What a way to go-go,' the camera operator said, 'Wait a minute. He said "What a way to go-go." ' I said, 'Yeah, I know,' and as I started to walk away, he walked up to me and said it again. Later, one of the guys on the show said that the crew didn't quite know what was going on, it was so crazy. The camera operator was trying to be helpful, figuring the guy blew the line and that I didn't notice."

BatFacts

- The scenes of the World's Fair used in this episode are in reality footage taken at the 1964–65 New York World's Fair.
- This is the only time Alfred wore a tuxedo throughout an entire episode.
- Dick Reeves (the Doorman) is best remembered for having played several villains on the old "Superman" TV series.
- In the May 1965 issue of the *Batman* comic, the Riddler, jealous of the attention Batman is giving to the Molehill Mob, arranges a trap so Batman will capture the gang giving the Riddler Batman's undivided attention. However, in this TV episode the Riddler teams up with the gang instead.

Special BatEquipment

Bathook
Antenna Activator
Antitheft Activator
Batostat Antifire Activator
Detect-a-scope
Homing Transmitter & Receiver
Emergency Batturn Lever
Batmobile Mobile Crime Computer
Universal Drug Antidote
Batlaser
U.S. & Canada Crime Computer
Batray Projector
Parachute Jettison Button
Batgauge

Trivia Quiz 1

What were the four different license plate numbers that appeared on the Batmobile during the run of the series?

3—Fine Feathered Finks
4—The Penguin's aJinx

Guest Cast

Penguin—Burgess Meredith
Dawn Robbins—Leslie Parrish
Sparrow—Walter Burke
Hawkeye—Lewis Charles
Mr. Jay—Dan Tobin
Warden Crichton—David Lewis
Jewelry Shop Owner—Alex D'Arcy
Assistant Shop Owner—Johnny Jacobs
Cellmate (Swoop)—Robert Phillips

Teleplay & story by Lorenzo Semple, Jr.
Directed by Robert Butler
Production # 8703
Original air dates: 1/19/66 & 1/20/66

Plot

Fine Feathered Finks. While awaiting release from prison, the rascally Penguin devises a scheme to get Batman to plan his next crimes for him. His first step is to attract Batman's attention. The Penguin has his Finks distribute free umbrellas to the patrons of a jewelry store and local bank. Once the customers are inside, the umbrellas explode, giving the Penguin's men perfect cover to commit a robbery, but not a single item is taken. A confused Commissioner Gordon calls in Batman.

The Caped Crusaders decide to pay a visit to the Penguin, who, under the alias K. G. Bird, now operates an umbrella factory. Penguin launches a giant umbrella (with the multicolored Batbrella—complete with Penguin's hidden transmitter—attached to the handle) from the roof of the factory. After the umbrella lands in the middle of the street, Batman batclimbs up to the handle and retrieves the Batbrella. Believing it to be a clue to the Penguin's next crime, Batman and Robin return with it to the Batcave to analyze it.

Unable to figure out the significance of the Batbrella, Batman, in his normal guise as Bruce Wayne, decides to plant a tiny transistorized microphone (disguised as a spider) in the Penguin's factory. Bruce soon finds himself trapped in a huge fishing net as the bug microphone sets off the Penguin's burglar alarm. Penguin, unaware of Bruce's identity, mistakes him for a spy from a rival umbrella factory, knocks him out, and orders his men to throw him into the furnace. Still entangled in the net, Bruce is tied down to a conveyor belt, which in a few moments will send him on a fiery trip into the 12,000-degree furnace.

The Penguin's a Jinx. Bruce revives just in time to retrieve his cigarette lighter, filled with a lifetime supply of compressed butane gas, from his pocket and throw it into the furnace. The furnace explodes. Bruce is thrown free of the net and makes his escape.

Later, while Penguin and his men eagerly eavesdrop, Batman and Robin decide that the Penguin is planning to kidnap the beautiful actress Dawn Robbins from her hotel penthouse apartment. Batman then maps out the Penguin's plot—just what the evil bird wanted.

Batman's plot works perfectly. The Penguin and his men swing across to Dawn Robbin's terrace on giant umbrellas. Penguin gasses the girl—suddenly Batman and Robin appear; they've bit the bait! Penguin's hidden magnet (on the terrace) drags the duo toward the wall, where they remain helpless.

Batman and Robin escape the magnet with the help of a passing bellboy [*Note:* Their escape is not shown—only mentioned.] and set a plan to trap the Penguin. Knowing Penguin is listening through the Batbrella bug, Batman arranges for the ransom money to be paid at Wayne Manor and announces that Robin and he will be hidden inside the suits of armor in the entrance hall. The Penguin delivers the actress to the manor and picks up the money, but not before gassing the suits of armor. The Penguin and his men return to the umbrella factory to divide up the money but find the Dynamic Duo waiting for them.

Actor Burgess Meredith (as told to journalist James H. Burns)

"It was a riotous experience. Everyone had a good time working together. We got to do an awful lot of ad-libbing. Mine usually came when the Penguin would insult Batman by calling him 'Batboob' or 'Bat-this' or 'Bat-that,' which made acting in the show additionally enjoyable. One funny item involved the fact that during the middle sixties I had already given up smoking for twenty to twenty-five years—but I had to smoke all the time as the Penguin. The smoke would get caught in my throat. Since I didn't want to constantly ruin takes by coughing out loud—which the smoke forced me to do—I developed the Penguin's 'quack, quack' to cover it. Actually, it was a pretty unlikely noise for the Penguin to make. I sounded more like a duck! The quack got so famous, though, that whenever the writers couldn't think of anything funny to put in their scripts, they'd write a 'quack, quack' for me. I also developed that little Penguin walk."

BatTalk
Director Robert Butler

"I remember thinking that 'Fine Feathered Finks' was the best one I did. It was great. Burgess was wonderful. I think the reason he was so good was because of that formal training, because what he did was formal theater really.

"I also remember thinking at the time, Why didn't the guys get the scale on the thickness of the giant umbrella handle correct? It's wimpy; it's too thin."

BatFacts

- The basis for this story came from a *Batman* comic book dated February 1965. The only real difference is that in the comic the Penguin steals the jeweled meteorite (which was mentioned in this story), instead of kidnapping Dawn Robbins (who does not appear in the comic story).

Special BatEquipment

Batzooka
Gotham City Plans & Views
Electronic Bugging Devices

Trivia Quiz 2

What is the name of the jewelry store seen in the first part of this episode?

5—THE JOKER IS WILD
6—BATMAN IS RILED

GUEST CAST

Joker—Cesar Romero
Queenie—Nancy Kovack
Museum Attendant (Mr. Hovis)—Jonathan Hole
Assistant Warden—Merritt Bohn
The Inebriate—Dick Curtis
Newscaster (Fred)—Jerry Dunphy
Henchman #1—Al Wyatt
Henchman #2—Angelo DeMeo

Teleplay & story by Robert Dozier
Directed by Don Weis
Production #8709
Original air dates: 1/26/66 & 1/27/66

PLOT

The Joker Is Wild. Upon learning that he is to be omitted from the Gotham City Museum of Modern Art's Comedian's Hall of Fame, the Joker escapes from jail to seek revenge. While in the process of looting the museum of its priceless jewel collection, the Joker and his men are surprised by Batman and Robin. A batfight ensues, and Batman is knocked unconscious. As the Joker's men carry the duo away, Batman recovers, and, with the help of a Batgas pellet from his utility belt, he captures the Joker's men while the Joker escapes through a trapdoor cleverly concealed in the floor.

The Joker returns to his amusement park hideout, where he creates his own utility belt. He then lures Batman and Robin to a live broadcast by the Gotham City Opera Company, where he and his men capture and threaten to unmask them on live television.

Batman Is Riled. As the Joker is about to remove Batman's mask, Batman manages once again to reach his utility belt and fire a small Batmissile, which triggers the sprinkler system. The Joker quickly responds with a smoke bomb and flees to the catwalk above the studio. Batman follows but is stopped by the Joker's snakelike trick streamers. The Joker makes his escape while Robin helps Batman untangle himself from the streamers.

Later, the Joker interrupts a television show to give Batman a clue to his next crime via a comical criminal game show. The clue leads the Dynamic Duo to the Last Longer Warehouse, where the Joker springs a trap. During the ensuing fight, the Joker switches Batman's utility belt for one of his own, so when Batman tries to stop him with a device from his belt, it backfires, and the Joker escapes.

Having defeated Batman, the Joker decides to steal the new steamship, the S.S. *Gotham*. He replaces the cork from the champagne bottle that will be used to christen the ship with one filled with paralyzing gas. On the day of the ceremony, Batman and Robin are chosen to christen the ship. Batman notices that the cork has been tampered with. Suspecting foul play, he and Robin take Universal Gas Antidote Pills prior to completing the christening. Batman then smashes the bottle, releasing the deadly gas. Everyone immediately collapses as the Joker's men carry the supposedly unconscious pair away. Back in his hideout, the Joker broadcasts an ultimatum using his tricky television camera. Either he is given title to the S.S. *Gotham* or he will behead Batman and Robin. Suddenly, the duo leap to their feet and subdue the astonished Joker and his men.

Actor Cesar Romero

"I was very surprised when the producer of the show called me and said that he was doing a series called 'Batman' and the important characters were the villains. They had done the first two with the Riddler and the Penguin with Frank Gorshin and Burgess Meredith, and now they were ready to do the third, and the villain was the Joker. He said, 'I would like you to play the part.' So, I said I would like to read the script and know what it is all about. So he said, 'Come on over to the studio, and I will show you the film of the first episode.' Of course, it was great. I said, 'Let me read this Joker part, and if it is as good as the first one, hell yes, I will do it.' So, I read the script, and I thought it was a gas, and I said, 'Sure, I'll do it.' "

BatTalk
Executive Producer William Dozier

"Jose Ferrer was my first choice for the Joker. He either didn't want to do it or couldn't. He has kicked himself ever since. 'Butch' Romero, whom I had known forever, was the second choice for the Joker, and I am not sure he did not turn out better than Jose. I am not sure that Jose would have captured the frivolity and the ludicrousness of the character. I think he may have taken himself a little too seriously as an actor to do that."

BatFacts

- The Joker's four henchmen that appeared at the beginning of this two-part episode were named after the following famous comedians: Stan Laurel, Oliver Hardy, W. C. Fields, and Ernie Kovacs.
- Episode writer Robert Dozier is the son of executive producer William Dozier.

HAA
AA!

EE

EE!

In New York, Batman's first two episodes earned the highest ratings since the Beatles visited "The Ed Sullivan Show."

Special BatEquipment

Hyperspectrographic Analyzer
Universal Drug Antidote Pill
Batgas pellet
Batmissile

Trivia Quiz 3

What was the name the Joker gave his villainous game show when he appeared on television?

7—Instant Freeze
8—Rats Like Cheese

GUEST CAST

Mr. Freeze—George Sanders
Princess Sandra—Shelby Grant
Chill—Troy Melton
Nippy—Guy Way
Mo—Roy Sickner
Paul Diamante—Robert Hogan
Mr. Perkins—William O'Connell
Kolevator (Butler)—John Zaremba
Art Rogers—Don Hannum
Al Scott—Ken Del Conte
Dr. Vince—Dan Terranova
Newscaster—John Willis
Photographer—Bill Hudson
Girl—Teri Garr

Teleplay & story by Max Hodge
Directed by Robert Butler
Production #8707
Original air dates: 2/2/66 & 2/3/66

PLOT

Instant Freeze. The cold-blooded Mr. Freeze plans his revenge against Batman, who accidentally spilled a beaker of Instant Freeze solution on him during a fight in his laboratory, thus condemning him to live out his life in an air-conditioned environment of fifty degrees below zero.

Mr. Freeze begins his rampage of revenge by stealing some famous diamonds ("ice" in the criminal world) from the Gotham City Diamond Exchange. When Batman and Robin arrive, he has six decoys of himself and six decoys of Batman appear, and the resulting confusion gives him enough time to escape.

Back in the Batcave, Batman comes to the conclusion that Mr. Freeze will next steal the Ghiaccio Circolo (Circle of Ice) diamond from the visiting Princess Sandra of Molino. They immediately rush to her hotel in order to save her from the frozen fiend. They arrive just as Mr. Freeze is making his escape and pursue him to the street, where he freezes them solid with his quick-freeze gun.

Rats Like Cheese. Our frozen heroes are immediately rushed to Gotham City Hospital's Super-Hypothermic-De-Icifier Chamber Mark VII, where the freezing process is reversed. Meanwhile, Mr. Freeze kidnaps the famous baseball player Paul Diamante (his name means "diamond" in Spanish). When Mr. Freeze realizes that Batman is still alive, he offers to release Diamante if Batman will agree to take his place as his prisoner.

Mr. Freeze keeps his word and releases Diamante at the same time that Batman is knocked unconscious and spirited away in a helicopter by Freeze's men. Robin, ordered by Batman to keep out of this entire affair, secretly follows Batman to Mr. Freeze's hideout, where he is captured by Freeze's men. After dinner, Mr. Freeze slowly changes the temperature of his hideout so that the duo will freeze to death. However, unknown to Mr. Freeze, Batman is wearing his super-thermo-B long underwear, which prevents him from being frozen long enough to knock Mr. Freeze out and reverse the temperature controls, quickly putting Mr. Freeze and his men on ice.

When Adam West was asked in 1966 how he could play such a kooky part so straight, he said: "The main thing I strive for is to overlay with style what is basically a pretty square character. You might say I'm trying to invest Dickensian surroundings with an Oscar Wilde flavor."

BatTalk
Director Robert Butler

"I remember thinking up the crooked angles to shoot villains' sequences. That was the thing that I took right from the comic books."

BatFacts

- Mr. Freeze's mode of transportation was an Amalgamated Ice Cream Company truck.
- Princess Sandra of Molino was also known as Sandra Carlson of Brooklyn.
- Dr. Vince was an obvious takeoff on the series "Ben Casey."
- This episode was one of the first television appearances of actress Teri Garr.
- The character of Mr. Freeze was based on a villain named Mr. Zero who first appeared in a February 1959 *Batman* comic book.
- George Sanders committed suicide on April 25, 1972.

Special BatEquipment

Super-Thermo-B Long Underwear
Antifreeze Capsule
Portable Freezing Chamber
Interdigital Batsorter
Giant Lighted Lucite Map of Gotham City

Trivia Quiz 4

What is Mr. Freeze's real name?

9—ZELDA THE GREAT
10—A DEATH
WORSE THAN FATE

GUEST CAST

Zelda—Anne Baxter
Eivol Ekdal—Jack Kruschen
Hillary Stonewin—Barbara Heller
Newsman—Frankie Darro
Officer Clancey—Jim Drum
Bank Guard—Stephen Tompkins
Hood #1—Victor French
Hood #2—Bill Phillips
Announcer—Jerry Doggett
Doctor—Douglas Dumbrille

Teleplay & story by Lorenzo Semple, Jr.
Directed by Norman Foster
Production #8705
Original air dates: 2/9/66 & 2/10/66

PLOT

Zelda the Great. Once a year, on April 1, exactly $100,000 is stolen from one of Gotham City's banks, and the identity of the thief remains a complete mystery. Actually, the thief is none other than Zelda the Great, a world-famous magician and escape artist who uses the stolen money to pay off her crooked escape device inventor, a strange Albanian genius named Eivol Ekdal.

Batman decides to set a trap for the unknown thief by having the local newspapers

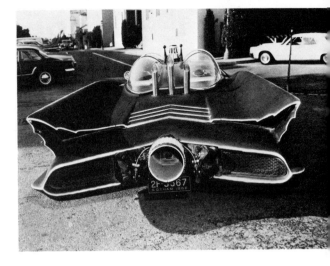

print a phony story stating that the money recently stolen from the bank was counterfeit. When Ekdal reads about the phony money, he refuses to give Zelda his latest invention, the Inescapable Doom-Trap, until he is paid. Noticing a story about a rare gem on display in a local jewelry store (which was also a phony story created by Batman), Ekdal decides to allow Zelda to pay for his new creation with the gem and sends her out to steal it. Zelda, realizing the gem could be a Batman trap, plans a counterattack. She kidnaps Aunt Harriet and encases her in a straitjacket suspended over a vat of boiling oil, then holds her for ransom.

A Death Worse Than Fate. Just as Zelda's deadline is about to run out, Bruce, Robin, and Commissioner Gordon appear on a live television broadcast and convince Zelda that the money she stole from the bank was real. Zelda releases Aunt Harriet, but not before placing a matchbook from Ekdal's Gnome Bookstore in Harriet's pocket. This clue she hopes will bring Batman into her trap.

The matchbook does its job, and Batman and Robin pay a visit to the bookstore, where they fall prey to Ekdal's inescapable Doom-Trap, a large transparent cage made out of Jet Age plastics. When a deadly helium-based gas fills the cage, Batman ignites it by placing his metal belt buckle against the electrified grating at the base of the cage. The resulting explosion opens the door, releasing them. Zelda, who had been watching from Ekdal's hidden control room, feels guilty and warns Batman about the gunmen hidden inside two mummy cases just outside the Doom-Trap waiting to kill them. Batman and Robin quickly duck out of the way as the gunmen accidentally kill each other. Just then, Ekdal tries to make a getaway but is quickly stopped by a well-thrown Batarang. Moments later, Zelda quietly gives up.

BATFACTS

- As Batman and Robin drive through Gotham City, the streets of New York's Times Square area can be seen in the background, including the two movie theaters playing *El Cid* and *Boys' Night Out*. These particular films were already three to four years old, so either Gotham City had difficulty getting new films or nobody bothered to check on the age of stock footage they were using.
- Victor French, best known for "Little House on the Prairie" and "Highway to Heaven," had a small role in this episode as a gangster sent to bump off Batman and Robin.
- This particular story was based on a story called "Batman's Inescapable Doom-Trap," which appeared in the December 1965 issue of *Detective Comics*. Although the character Eivol Ekdal appeared in the comic, Zelda did not. Instead, the magician was a man named Carnado.

SPECIAL BATEQUIPMENT

International Frequency Computer
Hyperspectrographic Analyzer

TRIVIA QUIZ 5

What was the name of the trick book Batman discovered at the Gnome Bookstore?

11—A Riddle a Day Keeps the Riddler Away
12—When the Rat's Away, the Mice Will Play

GUEST CAST

Riddler—Frank Gorshin
King Boris—Reginald Denny
Mousey—Susan Silo
Fangs—Marc Cavell
Whiskers—Tim Herbert
Whitey—Roy Jenson
Newsman—William Kendis
Julia Davis—Joy Harmon
M.C.—Johnny Magnus
Ambassador—Tris Coffin
Guest—John Archer
Maitre D'—John Hubbard
TV announcer—Marvin Miller

Teleplay & story by Fred De Gorter
Directed by Tom Gries
Production #8711
Original air dates: 2/16/66 & 2/17/66

PLOT

A Riddle a Day Keeps the Riddler
Away. Having survived the explosion in episode 2, the Riddler returns to upset ceremony once again. This time it is a welcoming ceremony for the visiting King Boris, who has arrived in Gotham City to present a gift from his country, a miniature replica of the Queen of Freedom Monument. The Riddler has his new female assistant, Mousey, present the King with an exploding bouquet of flowers. The explosion releases a hidden riddle, which leads Batman to believe that the Riddler is planning to steal the jeweled crown from the Miss Galaxy contest. Batman secretly replaces the crown with a fake one containing a miniature transmitter.

Later that night, the Riddler makes his appearance at the contest, steals the crown, and makes his escape down a trapdoor. Rushing outside to the waiting Batmobile, our heroes spot the Riddler hiding in an open manhole. He informs them that he knew the crown was a fake, at which point he throws the fake crown back to them and disappears down the hole. Upon closer examination, Batman discovers that the discarded crown contains another riddle.

This new riddle leads Batman to believe that the Riddler plans to kidnap the visiting King Boris. Unfortunately, Batman arrives too late to save the king from the clutches of the Prince of Puzzlers.

The Riddler plans to plant a time bomb inside the king's statue, which in turn will be placed inside the Gotham City Museum of Fame housed in the base of the towering monument.

Batman and Robin locate the Riddler's hideout but fall victim to the Riddler and his River Rat gang. They are subsequently strapped to a giant generator drive shaft and are about to be spun into oblivion.

BatFacts

- During the recap scene at the beginning of the second part of this episode, we are supposed to be shown a sketch of the Riddler's hideout at the waterworks, but instead we are shown the sketch of Dawn Robbins's penthouse apartment, which appeared in "Fine Feathered Finks."

  Apparently, whoever was in charge of the recap scene was not paying careful attention to details. Some of these episodes were so rushed, it's quite possible no one had time to review the show for goofs of this nature.
- Reginald Denny (King Boris) later went on to play his last role, that of Commodore Schmidlapp, in the Batman feature film.
- Marvin Miller is best known for the role of Michael Anthony on the series "The Millionaire."

When the Rat's Away, the Mice Will Play. While the Riddler's men escort King Boris and his statue back to the city, Batman manages to reach the blowtorch in his utility belt and burns the armature, causing a short circuit to occur, which deactivates the generator. Batman frees himself and Robin, and the duo return to the Batcave.

Believing he has destroyed our heroes, the Riddler proceeds with his blackmail scheme. Once King Boris has placed the statue inside the museum, the Riddler informs Commissioner Gordon that, unless he is paid $1,000,000, the Queen of Freedom monument will be destroyed.

Meanwhile, Batman has solved the Riddler's final riddle, figured out the Riddler's plan, and sets a trap for him inside the museum. The Riddler arrives to collect his money and finds not only that the statue with the bomb is missing but also that the satchel of money is a fake. Suddenly, Batman and Robin appear. They inform the Riddler that they have already deactivated the bomb and then proceed to deactivate the Riddler and his gang.

Special BatEquipment

Homing Receiverscope
Bat Blowtorch

Trivia Quiz 6

In this two-part episode, one of the Riddler's men dresses up in a Batman costume and pays a visit to Commissioner Gordon's office. Which henchman is he?

Guest Cast

Mad Hatter (Jervis Tetch)—David Wayne
Lisa—Diane McBain
Cappy—Roland La Starza
Dicer—Gil Perkins
Turkey Bullwinkle—George Conrad
Babette—Sandra Wells
Octave Marbot—Alberto Morin
Madame Magda—Monique Le Maire
Silver shop manager—Ralph Montgomery
Sporting goods manager—Bob Legionaire
Mrs. Monteagle—Norma Varden
Citizen—John Ward

Teleplay & story by Charles Hoffman
Directed by Norman Foster
Production #8719
Original air dates: 2/23/66 & 2/24/66

Plot

The Thirteenth Hat. Jervis Tetch, the Mad Hatter, sets out to take revenge against Batman and the twelve members of the jury that sent him to jail. Using the Super Instant Mesmerizer concealed in his high hat, he begins stealing the hats of the jurors along with their owners.

After collecting most of the jury, Tetch decides it is time to add Batman's cowl to his collection, so he sets a trap for Batman and Robin at the studio of sculptor Octave Marbot, who is currently sculpting a statue of Batman. Masquerading as Marbot, Tetch tries tricking Batman into removing his cowl so he can use it as a model for the head of the statue. Knowing full well that Marbot has already finished the statue's head, Batman suspects the sculptor is Tetch in disguise. Pretending to fall for Tetch's deception, Batman and Robin retire to the back room ostensibly to remove Batman's cowl. There they find the real Marbot tied up in the closet. They leave to confront Tetch. During the ensuing battle, the Mad Hatter manages to entomb poor Batman in Super-Fast Hardening Plaster.

Batman Stands Pat. After several minutes, Tetch is convinced that Batman has smothered to death inside the plaster, and he has the real Marbot break open the plaster so he can obtain a mold of Batman's cowl. As the sculptor slowly chips away at the plaster tomb, they become aware that someone is chipping away at the plaster

from the inside. Suddenly, Batman—who wisely held his Batbreath—breaks out of the plaster, and Tetch and his men make a hasty retreat.

Learning that Tetch has only one more juror to capture, Batman arranges for Alfred to plant a Homing Battransmitter inside the hat of Turkey Bullwinkle, the remaining juror, hoping that it will lead them to Tetch's hideout. Alfred manages to plant the device moments before Tetch and his assistant, Lisa, make off with Mr. Bullwinkle and his hat. Unfortunately, Tetch accidentally drops the hat, exposing the transmitter. Tetch decides to lure Batman into a trap.

Tetch deliberately leads the Caped Crusaders directly to his hideout, where he plans to use the ghoulish machinery of his hat factory to do away with our heroes. Batman and Robin fall into Tetch's trap but manage to outfight the fiend who falls into a vat of shrinking solution.

BATFACTS

- This episode is based on a February 1964 comic book story in which the Mad Hatter commits crimes based on the occupations of the jurors who sent him to prison.

SPECIAL BATEQUIPMENT

Batmobile Antitheft Device
Antimesmerizing Batreflector
International Frequency Computer
Anticrime Computer
Batresearch Shelf
Homing Battransmitter
Detect-a-scope

TRIVIA QUIZ 7

What was the name of the magazine that the Mad Hatter's assistant, Lisa, said she represented when she visited with Turkey Bullwinkle?

15—THE JOKER GOES TO SCHOOL
16—HE MEETS HIS MATCH,
THE GRISLEY GHOUL

GUEST CAST

Joker—Cesar Romero
Susie—Donna Loren
Nick—Kip King
Two-Bits—Greg Benedict
Schoolfield (principal)—Bryan O'Byrne
Pete—Tim O'Kelly
Cheerleader #1—Cherie Foster
Cheerleader #2—Linda Harrison
Vandergilt—Sydney Smith
Herbie—Glenn Allan
Third girl—Donna Di Martino
Joe—Dick Bellis
Fourth girl—Joan Parker
Cop—Breeland Rice
Fulton—Jim Henaghan

Teleplay & story by Lorenzo Semple, Jr.
Directed by Murray Golden
Production #8715
Original air dates: 3/2/66 & 3/3/66

HEE HAA HEE HEE! HAA! HEE!

PLOT

The Joker Goes to School. The Joker tries to undermine student morale at Woodrow Roosevelt High School in order to recruit high school dropouts for his gang of Bad Pennies. He carries out his plan by rigging the school vending machines to give out silver dollars instead of containers of milk.

Unknown to everyone, the school's head cheerleader, Susie, is actually a member of the Joker's gang. She arranges to steal some important school exam papers so the Joker can use them in a blackmail scheme. She also leads the Dynamic Duo into a trap set by the Joker.

The Joker captures the duo via one of the rigged vending machines, but instead of giving out silver dollars this machine locks them in leg irons and then emits knockout gas. Batman and Robin are then transferred to the inside of a moving van, where they are tied to electric chairs. On the wall is a slot machine, which when activated will release 50,000 volts of electricity if the machine turns up three lemons.

He Meets His Match, the Grisley Ghoul.

Just as the slot machine turns up its third lemon, Gotham City suffers a massive blackout. The Joker and his gang flee, as the police arrive just in time to release the duo from the electric chairs before the power is restored.

After replaying the audio tape Batman secretly made while in the van, they were able to identify Susie as one of the Joker's gang members. So, Robin, in the guise of Dick Grayson, tries to trick Susie into leading him to the Joker. Unfortunately, gang member Nick catches on to Dick's plan and sends him on his way.

Realizing that Batman knows that Susie is one of the gang, the Joker gives her some perfume, which he instructs her to use only after she has planted the answers to those important exam papers she stole inside one of the rigged vending machines. She doesn't know the perfume has been poisoned.

Batman and Robin save Susie from the poisoned perfume, and in return she informs them of the Joker's plan. Meanwhile, the Joker and his gang arrive at the school just in time to photograph the school basketball team holding the answers to the exams. He now plans to use the photo to have the team disqualified for cheating, thus preventing them from playing in the big game. You see, the Joker bet his money on the other team, and with the top players out of the game the opposing team from Disko Tech would win.

Batman and Robin suddenly swing down from the rafters on their Batropes to inform the students that they have switched the test answers and the ones the Joker photographed were fakes. They then proceed to put the Joker and his Bad Pennies out of circulation.

BatTalk
Executive Producer William Dozier

"In England, kids started jumping out of windows; they thought Batman could fly. They thought the cape was wings. We had to do a special lead-in to the show, with an interview with Batman saying, 'Boys and girls, I do not fly. I can't fly any better than you can. Don't think I can and don't think you can. And don't take chances by trying to jump off the roof.' They were doing it, but never in this country. Thank heaven it never started in this country."

BatFacts

- Linda Harrison, who played one of this episode's cheerleaders, later went on to play Nova in the film *Planet of the Apes*. She also happened to be married to 20th Century-Fox president Darryl Zanuck at the time.
- The Joker's hideout was at the One Armed Bandit Novelty Company.

During the first day of shooting, the Batmobile went out of control and nearly obliterated the star who had his foot caught in the brake.

Special BatEquipment

Batscope
Micro-TV Camera
Anticrime Voice Analyzer
Voice File
Anticrime Auxiliary Generator
Anti-Allergy Pill
Remote Radio Pickup

Trivia Quiz 8

What was the name of the Joker's bookie?

17—TRUE OR FALSE-FACE
18—HOLY RAT RACE

GUEST CAST

False-Face—Malachi Throne
Blaze—Myrna Fahey
Burns (Midget)—Billy Curtis
Brinks (Fat Man)—Joe Brooks
Pinkerton (Thin Man)—Chuck Fox
Mr. Ladd—S. John Launer
Curator—Patrick Whyte
Cowboy—Mike Ragan
Leo Gore—Michael Fox
TV Announcer—Gary Owens

Teleplay & story by Stephen Kandel
Directed by William A. Graham
Production #8713
Original air dates: 3/9/66 & 3/10/66

PLOT

True or False-Face. The master of disguise, False-Face, manages to steal the jeweled Mergenberg Crown and replace it with a false one right under the watchful eyes of the police. Included with the false crown is a note that leads Batman to believe that False-Face is planning to rob an armored car. Batman catches False-Face, who is disguised as one of the armored car drivers but manages to escape in his Trick-Truck.

Batman and Robin follow False-Face into an alley, where they are attacked by False-Face's gang. The police arrive in time to arrest the gang, but False-Face escapes by disguising himself as Chief O'Hara. Batman captures False-Face's assistant, Blaze, who leads the duo to what they think is False-Face's hideout, a deserted subway platform. It is in reality a False-Face trap. Batman is gassed by a vending machine while Blaze gasses Robin. They awake to find that False-Face has glued them to the train tracks with a super-strong epoxy. Momentarily, they will be run over by a speeding train.

Holy Rat Race. As our heroes await their approaching doom, faithful Alfred contacts his employer on the Battransmitter in response to a broadcasted radio message sent by Blaze. Batman orders Alfred to throw the short-circuit lever of the Battransmitter, which causes Batman's radio to explode, melting the epoxy on his wrist that allows him to reach the Batlaser in his utility belt, which he uses to melt away the remaining epoxy, freeing himself and Robin just as the train passes through the station.

Returning to the commissioner's office, they deduce that False-Face is planning to flood Gotham City with millions of dollars in counterfeit money. No one will be able to tell the real money from the false money. The only money that will be any good will be the money False-Face stole from the bank.

Batman manages to surprise False-Face and his gang as they try to break into the bank vault. False-Face escapes to his hideout at the old Bioscope Movie Studios in his Trick-Truck, where with Blaze's help and a false inflatable Batmobile, False-Face is finally captured.

BatTalk

Actor Malachi Throne

"Originally False-Face was to be done with makeup, but due to production problems or decisions a plastic mask was used instead. It was a good character, but the problem was that the mask came out rather ugly and uncomical when photographed. The mask was bad, and it prevented the character from repeating because there was no response to the character. Although I felt my work was good, it would have been better had they stuck to the original concept—different facial disguises.

"Also, the concept of False-Face's not being headlined was my idea. The question mark in the credits was the producer's choice, but during a contractual argument I insisted that my name be withdrawn from the credits since there was going to be no face on it and no real acting. I was irate enough to say, 'Anyone could have played that part behind that kind of a mask, so please withdraw my name from the credits.' In the meantime, a huge bunch of publicity arose from that with regard to what had leaked out—not with regard to me, but with regard to whether Frank Sinatra was playing the part, or Sammy Davis was playing the part, or Cary Grant, because everything was so celebrity-conscious during the early days of 'Batman.' So, everybody in town was having a good time guessing who was playing False-Face.

"As for riding the motorcycle, I only got off on a start. I didn't do any of the actual stunts. Many of the ideas, in terms of what the character was doing and how to do it, like the hands and the gloves, were mine. For the gloves, I borrowed W. C. Fields's crooks and turns of the fingers.

"They were going to use Angie Dickinson for the part of Blaze, because everybody was dying to be on that show and to play any part. Director Billy Graham cast me in it even though I was not on the same name level as some of the other people. That was like a coup, but they pulled the rug out from under me with that stupid mask."

BatFacts

- During the scene at the Bioscope Movie Studios in which Chief O'Hara drives up to the false inflatable Batmobile, if you look into his rearview mirror, you can see the cameraman, who was in the back seat of the car.
- This episode was based on a June 1958 comic book story.

Special BatEquipment

Intergalactic Recorder
Short-Circuit Lever of the Battransmitter
Batanalyzer
False Inflatable Batmobile
Bat Alarm
Wrist Batradio

Trivia Quiz 9

a. What train was about to run over Batman and Robin?

b. What was the message Blaze had broadcasted over the radio?

19—The Purr-fect Crime
20—Better Luck Next Time

Guest Cast

Catwoman—Julie Newmar
Leo—Jock Mahoney
Felix—Ralph Manza
Mr. Andrews—Harry Holcomb
Guard—Pat Zurica
Henchman—Alex Sharp

Teleplay & story by Stanley Ralph Ross & Lee Orgel
Directed by James Sheldon
Production #8721
Original air dates: 3/16/66 & 3/17/66

Plot

The Purr-fect Crime. The Catwoman purloins one of a matched pair of priceless golden cat statues (which hold the secret to the lost treasure of Captain Manx) from the collection of Mark Andrews, leading Batman to believe that the remaining statue will be her next target. Coating the cat with radioactive mist, the duo wait in the shadows for Catwoman to appear. But the sneaky feline manages to drug Robin, and, while Batman is tending to the unconscious boy, she and her men make their escape with the cat.

After Robin revives, the duo use the Batometer to follow Catwoman's trail left by the radioactive mist. The trail leads them to the Gato & Chat Fur Company at 2809 West 20th Street, where they fall through a trapdoor into Catwoman's clutches. After subjecting her prey to a moving wall of spikes (made of rubber) and a toy bomb, as cats will do, she removes Robin and leaves Batman to choose his own fate. In front of him are two doors; Catwoman is behind one of them, but behind the other is a huge Batman-eating tiger. Naturally, Batman chooses the wrong door, and out leaps the tiger.

Better Luck Next Time. Batman fends off the tiger long enough to remove his Batclaws from his utility belt. Using the claws, he climbs up the wall and out of the reach of the tiger. Realizing that he won't be able to stay up there forever, he removes his Batearplugs from his belt and places them on either side of his cowl, then adjusts his Batcommunicator to emit 20,000 decibels of high-pitched sound, which subdues the tiger. Batman leaps from the wall and takes refuge in the room from which the tiger was released. He soon finds himself lost in the catacombs of Catwoman's lair.

Meanwhile, Catwoman has Robin balanced on the end of a board over a pit of hungry tigers, and at the other end of the board is a supply of sand exactly equal to Robin's weight. As the sand is released, the board will slowly lower Robin into the tiger's den. Leaving her henchmen to carry out the dirty work, the Catwoman goes off in search of the lost treasure of Captain Manx.

Batman locates Robin in the nick of time, and the two battle the Catwoman's henchmen. During the fight, the Catwoman's chief henchman, Leo, escapes to warn Catwoman that Batman is on her tail. Catwoman then has Leo mine the road leading to the cave where the treasure is hidden. But thanks to the Batmobile Batarmor and Automatic Tire Repair Device, they survive the explosions.

While Batman battles the mine field, Catwoman and Leo locate the treasure. Greed getting the better of her, she gasses Leo and escapes into the depths of the cave just as the Dynamic Duo arrive. They chase her to the edge of a bottomless crevice, which she attempts to jump. With the heavy booty pulling her down, she barely manages to grab on to the other side. Rather than drop the treasure to save one of her lives, she plunges into the dark pit below.

Actress Julie Newmar

"I had lived in New York at the time on Beekman Place. I remember it was a weekend, Friday or Saturday, and my brother had come down from Harvard with five or six of his friends, and we were all sitting around the sofa, just chatting away, when the phone rang. I got up and answered it, and it was this agent or someone in Hollywood, who said, 'Miss Newmar, would you like to play the Catwoman on the "Batman" series? They are casting it out here.' I was insulted because he said, 'It starts Monday.' I said, 'What is this?' That's how television is done: they never know what they are doing until yesterday. My brother leapt off the sofa. I mean he physically levitated and said, 'Batman! That's the favorite show at Harvard. We all quit our classes and quit our studies and run into the TV room and watch this show.' I said, 'They want me to play Catwoman.' He said, 'Do it!' So, I said, 'OK, I'll do it.' "

BatTalk
Actor Joey Tata

Joey was an occasional actor on the show and visited the set during this episode.

"The giant Bengal tiger went berserk during the shooting, bit a cable, and was severely shocked. I don't know if the cat died or not. But it was awful; it just went nuts."

BatFacts

- The address used for the Gato and Chat Fur Company was actually the former Brooklyn home address of writer Stanley Ralph Ross.
- "Gato" is Spanish for "cat"; "Chat" is French for "cat."
- In the comics, Catwoman's real name was Selina Kyle, but it was never used on the TV series.
- There was actually only one live tiger used on the show; the others in the pit were stock footage.

Special BatEquipment

Safety BatBelt
Auxiliary Power Channel
Anticrime Voice Analyzer
Batometer
Radioactive Mist
Universal Drug Antidote Pills
Batbeam
Batclaws
Batearplugs
Batcommunicator
Metal Analyzer
Spectrascope
Batresearch shelf
Batmobile Batarmor
Automatic Tire Repair Device

Trivia Quiz 10

a. What was the name of the tiger?
b. Exactly how much did Robin weigh?

21—THE PENGUIN GOES STRAIGHT
22—NOT YET, HE AIN'T

CAST

Penguin—Burgess Meredith
Sophia Starr—Kathleen Crowley
Eagle-Eye—Harvey Lembeck
Dove—Al Checco
Mrs. Van Climber—Hope Sansberry
Crook—Ed McCready
Lt. Copple—Douglas Bank
Reggie Rich—William Beckley
Newsman (George)—Bill Welch
Cop (Clancy)—Jim Drum

Teleplay & story by Lorenzo Semple, Jr. &
  John Cardwell
Directed by Leslie H. Martinson
Production #8723
Original air dates: 3/23/66 & 3/24/66

PLOT

The Penguin Goes Straight. While attending a matinee performance at a Gotham City theater, the Penguin, with the aid of his bulletproof umbrella, prevents a crook from robbing the beautiful actress Sophia Starr. Later, at the Millionaire's Club, Penguin once again prevents a crime, this time stopping two crooks (actually Penguin's own Finks) from abducting millionaire Reggie Rich from a steam room. When Batman and Robin finally arrive at the club, they learn the Penguin has now opened his own Penguin Protective Agency, which will protect the wealth of Gotham City's society crowd, including Sophia Starr's jewelry.

In an attempt to prevent Penguin from stealing Miss Starr's jewelry, Batman has Alfred pose as an insurance company agent sent to photograph the jewelry. Aside from photographing the jewelry, Alfred must also switch the Penguin's cigarette holder for one containing a hidden microphone. When the Penguin discovers the switch, Alfred manages to escape with the photos by pulling the rug out from under the Penguin.

That night, Batman and Robin break into Miss Starr's apartment in order to replace the real jewelry with fakes they have made based on Alfred's photos. They are caught making the switch by the Penguin and his Finks, who accuse them of burglary. The duo manage to escape but are now labeled fugitives from justice.

When the Penguin throws a party at the Gotham City Amusement Pier, the Caped Crusaders arrive to investigate. They quickly fall into a Penguin trap and find themselves strung up behind a shooting gallery, with Commissioner Gordon and Chief O'Hara about to fire at them with umbrella guns loaded with real bullets.

Not Yet, He Ain't. Just as Gordon and O'Hara fire the guns, Batman and Robin lift up their feet, so that the bulletproof soles of their boots deflect the deadly bullets. Batman then cuts them both free with his Batknife. When Penguin discovers they have escaped, he gets his new society friends to put pressure on Gordon to arrest the duo.

Faking insanity, Batman and Robin arrive at the Penguin Protective Agency ready to kill the Penguin, who calls in the police. After chasing the duo for a few blocks, the police trap the two in a deserted alley where they appear to gun down the berserk pair. (The police were really firing blank cartridges, as Batman had planned.)

Believing our heroes are dead, Penguin steals the Batmobile and races off to plan his latest caper, the theft of the valuable wedding gifts from his own wedding to Sophia Starr.

Penguin and his Finks use exploding waterpipes and trick umbrellas to cover up their theft of the priceless wedding gifts. They then make their escape in the Batmobile (now, of course, the Birdmobile). Following close behind in the Batcycle, Batman and Robin use the Batmobile's remote control devices to stop the Penguin and his men.

BatTalk

Actor Burgess Meredith (as told to journalist James H. Burns)

"I did 'Batman' for two reasons, one of which was salary. The other was that, after its first few episodes, 'Batman' became the in-thing to do. Everybody, including Frank Sinatra, would either play a villain or appear as himself in that cameo showcase where a celebrity would poke his head through the window of a building that Batman and Robin were climbing. I even remember Otto Preminger saying to me, 'My God, my son won't speak to me unless I get a job on "Batman." ' Eventually, he got in! Actually, we didn't get as much money from the show as you might think, although we were paid decent money

for the feature film version. The main impetus to continue appearing on 'Batman'—beyond the desire to get some TV work—was that it was fashionable."

BatFacts

- While the Batmobile is driving down the streets of Gotham City, you can spot the famous Schwab's Drugstore, which is (or was) in Los Angeles.
- Harvey Lembeck is best known for his portrayal of the comical Eric Von Zipper in the beach party movies of the 1960s.

Special BatEquipment

Electric Eye Looping Unit
Batmobile's Bulletproof Windshield
Batknife
Remote Control Batmobile Ejector Button
Batscanner

Trivia Quiz 11

What was the name of the insurance company Alfred told the Penguin he represented?

23—THE RING OF WAX
24—GIVE 'EM THE AXE

GUEST CAST

Riddler—Frank Gorshin
Tallow—Joey Tata
Matches—Michael Greene
Moth—Linda Gaye Scott
Madame Soleil—Ann Ayars
Miss Prentice—Elizabeth Harrower
Mayor—Al McGranary

Teleplay & story by Jack Paritz & Bob Rodgers
Directed by James B. Clark
Production #8725
Original air dates: 3/30/66 & 3/31/66

PLOT

The Ring of Wax. The Riddler smuggles a Universal Wax Solvent into the country inside a wax statue of Batman intended for display at Madame Soleil's Wax Museum. In place of the Batman statue is a wax replica of the Riddler, which at its unveiling sprays the audience with a paint gun while a tape recorder issues two riddles.

The riddles lead Batman and Robin to the Gotham City Public Library, where the Riddler has broken into the rare book vault with his new wax solvent to steal a book about the lost treasure of the Incas. When the duo arrive at the library, the Riddler is ready for them. Using a can of wax emulsion spray, he glues them to the floor, and he and his men make their escape with the book.

The duo track their enemies back to the wax museum, where they are captured by the Riddler and his gang. The Riddler takes them back to his hideout at the Kandle Lite Candle Factory, where he plans to turn them into giant candles by dipping them into a huge vat of boiling wax.

Give 'em the Axe. While the fumes from molten wax cause the Riddler and his gang to take refuge downstairs, Batman manages to reflect a single ray of sun off his highly polished belt buckle into an open barrel of highly explosive chemicals. The subsequent explosion throws the pair free of the boiling wax but also knocks them unconscious. Believing the explosion killed them, the Riddler races off to the Gotham City Museum in search of the Incan treasure.

After having recovered from the blast the duo trace the Riddler to the museum but find the museum doors locked. The only entrance seems to be a small window on an upper floor. As Batman is too big to fit through it, Robin is elected to climb through and open the door for Batman. While on his way through the building, Robin meets up with the Riddler's henchmen, who overpower him and bring him to the Riddler, who has him tied down and stretched on a medieval rack.

Batman suspects that Robin is in trouble and uses the Batram on the Batmobile to break into the museum. Batman arrives in time to rescue Robin, defeat the Riddler and his gang, and prevent the Universal Wax Solvent from destroying a rare old sarcophagus containing an Incan mummy and the missing treasure.

BatFacts

- Actress Linda Gaye Scott is the heiress to the Scott paper company.
- This episode apparently takes place prior to the election of Mayor Linseed, as a different mayor is in office at the time of the story.

BatTalk
Actor Joey Tata

"Gorshin and I stole the Batmobile once. We had this running shot, where we would get into the Batmobile and just take off. That was the cut, but we kept going and kept laughing. Frank says, 'Do you believe this? Where are we going to go with this?' I said, 'Why don't we use all of the lines? You'll say, "Hi, park this." No one will question us because you have question marks all over your green underwear and I am walking around with this pasty look on my face.' But we never did leave the studio."

Special BatEquipment

Batlaser Gun
Ultrasonic Indicator
Hyperspectrographic Analyzer
Batram

Trivia Quiz 12

What was the full name of the Riddler's wax emulsion spray?

GUEST CAST

Joker—Cesar Romero
Jill—Jane Wald
Maharajah—Dan Seymour
Mr. Prescott Belmont—Tol Avery
Mrs. Belmont—Angela Greene
Lookout—Norman Alden
Mayor Linseed—Byron Keith
Henchman #2—Johnny Seven
Girl Clerk—Bebe Louie

Teleplay & story by Francis & Marian Cockrell
Directed by Richard C. Sarafian
Production #8727
Original air dates: 4/6/66 & 4/7/66

PLOT

The Joker Trumps an Ace. The Clown Prince of Crime, the Joker, returns to commit what appear to be two senseless crimes. First he raids a fur salon, where he steals a hairpin from one of the rich patrons. Then he steals one of the holes from a golf course. Batman and Robin are called in to investigate, arriving at Gordon's office just as an inflatable jack-in-the-box sent by the Joker is delivered. Batman deduces that the Joker plans to steal the solid gold golf clubs belonging to the visiting Maharajah of Nimpah and immediately rushes down to the golf course to thwart the villain.

Just as the maharajah hits the golf ball into the hole he is playing, a cloud of colored gas spumes from it, immobilizing everyone. (As it turns out, this is the hole the Joker stole. He used the stolen hairpin as a trigger, and when it was struck by the golf ball, the smoke bomb concealed in the hole was activated.) The Joker's men then move in with a forklift (as the royal fellow weighs over 350 pounds) and carry the unconscious maharajah to a waiting van. The Caped Crusaders run quickly to the Batmobile to give pursuit. Just as they are about to close in, the van, which is covered with folding mirrors that allow it to blend completely into the background, disappears.

Later, the duo trace the funny fiend to his headquarters at the abandoned Katz, Katz, Katz & Co. Oil Refinery, where they are captured and locked inside an enormous chimney, which is then filled with a deadly gas.

BatFacts

- At the end of the episode, Batman is rumored to be running for the office of governor of California.
- Actor Dan Symour (whose names is mispelled in the credits as *Seymore*) is best remembered for playing many of the villains on the old "Superman" TV show.

Batman Sets the Pace. Realizing the only way they are going to escape the slowly rising gas is to go straight up the wall, the duo press their backs together for support and climb up the wall to the opening above. The Joker and his men escape just as Batman and Robin emerge from the chimney.

Back in the Batcave, Batman analyzes the traces of gas left inside the hole at the golf course and discovers that the gas used during the kidnap can be obtained only at the Ferguson Novelty and Magician's Supply Company. Visiting the novelty company in their normal identities as Bruce and Dick, they discover that it is actually being used as a front for the Joker and that the maharajah is hidden there. Later that night, dressed once again as Batman and Robin, they pay a surprise visit to the novelty company, where they capture several of the Joker's men, although the Joker manages to escape. After further investigation they discover that the maharajah is nowhere to be found.

Later, the Joker calls Commissioner Gordon, who subsequently puts Batman on the line and demands $500,000 in ransom money in exchange for the safe return of the maharajah. He also wants Batman to endorse the maharajah's personal check (the maharajah is paying the ransom with his own money) for that amount, which he will cash at the Gotham City State Bank the following morning.

Morning comes, and when the maharajah arrives to collect the money Batman exposes him as the Joker in disguise. Concerned that no one protested the kidnapping of the maharajah, Batman had called Nimpah and discoverd that the real maharajah had been away on a hunting trip all the time.

BURT WARD FACTS (ACCORDING TO SIDNEY SKOLSKY):
- He split a brick and a board in two as part of the "Batman" audition.
- He was featured in Ripley's "Believe It or Not" as the world's youngest professional ice skater when he was two.
- He pitched several no-hitters in the L.A. Municipal Baseball League when he was 13.
- His real name was Bert John Gervis ("Ward was my mother's maiden name").

Special BatEquipment

Retrorockets
Metal Analyzer
Hyperspectrographic Analyzer

Trivia Quiz 13

What name and slogan were printed on the truck the Joker used to kidnap the maharajah?

41

27—The Curse of Tut
28—The Pharoah's in a Rut

Guest Cast

King Tut—Victor Buono
Nefertiti—Ziva Rodann
Grand Vizier—Don "Red" Barry
Royal Scrivener—Frank Christi
Board Member—Bill Quinn
Reporter—Emanuel Thomas
Policeman—Bill Boyett
Newscaster—Olan Soule

Teleplay & story by Robert C. Dennis & Earl
  Barret
Directed by Charles R. Rondeau
Production #8729
Original Air dates— 4/13/66 & 4/14/66

Plot

The Curse of Tut. The nefarious King Tut plans to take over Gotham City, which he believes to be the modern-day version of ancient Thebes, and make it his own. From a giant sphinx deposited in Gotham Central Park, he begins making his demands, which include the demise of Batman and Robin.

After a fight with King Tut's men (or Tutlings, as the pharoah calls them) Batman, as Bruce Wayne, plans a trap for the over-stuffed monarch at the Gotham Museum's new Egyptian exhibit, but Tut turns the tables on him, and Bruce is kidnapped for ransom by a pair of Tutlings dressed as ambulance drivers. Bruce is then strapped to a gurney and loaded into the back of an ambulance, which begins its journey up a winding road. During a sharp turn, the gurney breaks out of the ambulance, leading Bruce on a treacherous ride that will end in a 300-foot drop off the side of a cliff.

The Pharoah's in a Rut. Just as the gurney is about to go over the cliff, Bruce manages to free himself from the straps and grab on to a guard rail, saving himself from certain doom.

Upon learning of Wayne's escape, Tut arranges another kidnapping. Believing Batman is away in Egypt doing research, he sends his men to Wayne Manor to carry out his plan. Batman, with the aid of a life-like replica of Bruce, tricks the Tutlings into taking him to Tut. While en route to the hideout in the Royal Bark, Batman is discovered and knocked unconscious. Later, at the hideout, Batman and Tut's disloyal queen are subjected to the ancient Theban pebble torture.

Meanwhile, Robin has traced the Royal Bark to the old Egyptian Pavilion left over from last year's Gotham City World's Fair, which Tut is using as a hideout. Knowing that he is too young to drive the Batmobile, the Boy Wonder enlists Alfred's aid in rescuing Batman.

Tut believes that the pebble torture has unhinged Batman's mind, so he orders Batman to dance for him (to Batmusic, of course). Unbeknownst to Tut, Batman saved his sanity by reciting the multiplication tables backward. As Batman is about to rout Tut and his henchmen, Robin arrives to lend a hand. During the fight, Tut escapes, overpowers Alfred, and makes off with the Batmobile. The duo and Alfred pursue the villain in the Royal Bark.

Using his Batcommunicator, Batman activates the Voice-Control Batmobile Relay Circuit in the Batcave in the hopes of activating the Batmobile's ejection seat. However, just as he issues the orders, the radio goes dead. To make matters worse, Tut has discovered the deadly Batbeam and doubles back in an attempt to destroy the Dynamic Duo. Fortunately for our heroes, a short circuit activates the ejection seat instead of the Batbeam, sending Tut flying through the air to bounce off the Royal Bark and land at Batman's feet. The Caped Crusader quickly knocks him out. Later, in the Commissioner's office, Tut surprises everyone when he awakens as his former scholarly self.

BatFacts

- Actor Olan Soule who portrays the newscaster in this episode is better known to Batman fans as the voice of the animated Batman.
- The "Batman" cover issue of *TV Guide* announced that Robert Morley was scheduled to play King Tut, which turned out to be completely unfounded.

BatTalk
Executive Producer William Dozier

"Between [producer] Howie Horwitz and me, we just decided that Buono looked the part of a big Arab king. He was marvelous, and so was that beard. Although the part was not created for him, we knew he was Tut as soon as we saw him."

Special BatEquipment

Antigas Pill
Batscanner Receiver
Emergency Backup Receivers
Giant Lighted Lucite Map of Gotham City
Gotham City Plans & Views
Batmobile's Super-power Afterburner
Batbeam Firing Button
Voice-Control Batmobile Relay Circuit
Batmobile Ejection Seat

Trivia Quiz 14

a. How did the professor originally become the evil King Tut?

b. In what manner was he supposed to have died?

29—THE BOOKWORM TURNS
30—WHILE GOTHAM CITY BURNS

GUEST CAST

Bookworm—Roddy McDowall
Lydia Limpet—Francine York
Printer's Devil—John Crawford
Typesetter—Jan Peters
Pressman—Tony Aiello
Mayor Linseed—Byron Keith
Sergeant—Jim O'Hara
Cameo (window)—Jerry Lewis

Teleplay & story by Rik Vollaerts
Directed by Larry Peerce
Production #8717
Original Air Dates: 4/20/66 & 4/21/66

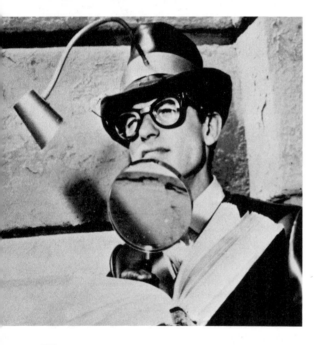

PLOT

The Bookworm Turns. In order to lure Batman and Robin to police headquarters, the Bookworm, the notorious master of stolen book plots, arranges a phony assassination of Commissioner Gordon during the dedication ceremony of the new Amerigo Columbus Bridge. Once the duo enter the police headquarters, the Bookworm has his assistant, Lydia Limpet, plant an exploding book on the front seat of the Batmobile. After having discovered that Gordon is very much alive, Batman is alerted by the Batmobile's Bomb Detector of the impending doom and presses the Batmobile's Radio Controlled Ejector Button, causing the exploding book to detonate in midair. They quickly return to the Batmobile to discover a clue in the form of the cover of the exploding book. Back at the Batcave, they deduce from the book cover that Bookworm is planning to blow up the new bridge. And blow up the bridge he does, into a huge photo on the side of a building.

Our heroes trace the photo back to a giant projector mounted on top of an abandoned bookmobile, and on closer inspection they discover Miss Limpet bound and gagged inside. Believing she is part of a Bookworm trap, they take her back to the Batcave (after knocking her out with Batsleep), where they hope the Hypermetric Lie-Detector will help them learn the Bookworm's plan.

After learning what they can from Lydia, they return her to the bookmobile, where Batman activates the trap. Leaving Robin behind to guard her, Batman pretends to race off on the trail of Lydia's false clues. Using a trick book, Lydia gasses Robin and calls for the Bookworm.

The Bookworm and his men transport Robin to Wayne Memorial Clock Tower, where they tie him to the clapper of the giant bell. When the clock strikes midnight in a few minutes, the bell will begin to toll the hour. The Bookworm departs, leaving Robin to be "rung" out.

While Gotham City Burns. Recalling a statement made by Miss Limpet ("he strikes at midnight"), Batman heads for the clock tower, where he and Chief O'Hara (whom he had met along the way) attempt to stop the clock before it is too late. After O'Hara fails to shoot out the clock's mechanism, with only a minute left until midnight, Batman uses the Batzooka to shoot a line to the lightning rod on top of the tower and then a second line to the hands of the clock. He then connects the ends of the lines to the Batmobile's nuclear power source, both into the postive terminal, which hopefully will cause the clapper and the bell to become positively charged and thus to repel each other. Just as the clapper is about to strike, Batman's plan works and Robin is saved.

Bookworm tries again. After stealing a rare cookbook from Wayne Manor, he arranges for a giant-sized cookbook to appear in the middle of a city street. The duo race to the scene and soon find themselves trapped inside the armor-plated book as scalding hot steam is pumped in!

Meanwhile, Bookworm heads in the Batmobile for the Morganbilt Library, where he plans to use the Batbeam to break into the Library and steal all of the rare and priceless books it holds.

As the police attempt to open the giant cookbook, Batman contacts the Batcave and, with Alfred's help, locates the manhole under the book from which the Bookworm introduced the steampipe. It is through this opening that the Caped Crusaders make their escape.

After picking up the Bookworm's conversation in the Batmobile via a concealed microphone, Batman and Robin head to the Library, where they capture the demented plagiarist and his entire gang.

BatTalk

Actor Roddy McDowall

"It was a show that everyone wanted to do at that period. It was such fun. They were larger-than-life cartoon characters, which are very interesting to play.

"I loved being part of the whole series. The costume, though, was very hot to wear. It was a wonderful part. I think there was talk about doing three episodes, but I don't know what happened, because there was only one segment. I don't know whether they changed their minds about the Bookworm or whether I was doing other things."

BatFact

- In many TV trivia and TV information books, it is often stated that actress Joan Crawford portrayed the assistant to the Bookworm, the Devil. This error occurred when one book accidentally mispelled actor John Crawford's name. Many subsequent books then apparently used this particular volume for reference without questioning the listing. In fact, even an arcade trivia machine uses this misinformation. So, to set the record straight, Joan Crawford never appeared on "Batman," as the Devil or as anything else.

Special BatEquipment

Batmobile Bomb Detector
Batmobile Radio Controlled Ejector Button
Batmobile Parachute Pickup Service
Ultrasonic Batray
Hypermetric Lie-Detector
Mobile Batphone
Laser-Beam Cutting Torch
High-Energy Radar
Batmagnet
Anticrime Computer
Gotham City Plans and Views

Trivia Quiz 15

a. What was the name of the giant cookbook the Bookworm used to trap the Dynamic Duo?

b. What was the name of the book with which the Bookworm was going to hit Miss Limpet over the head?

c. What was the name of the book that almost exploded inside the Batmobile?

31—DEATH IN SLOW MOTION
32—THE RIDDLER'S FALSE NOTION

GUEST CAST

Riddler—Frank Gorshin
Pauline—Sherry Jackson
C.B.—Richard Bakalyan
Van Bloheim—Theo Marcuse
Wolf—Burt Brandon
Van Jones—Francis X. Bushman
Theatre Manager—Walter Woolf King
Guard—Alex Bookston
Sylvia—Virginia Wood
Cashier—Judy Pace

Teleplay and story by Dick Carr
Directed by Charles R. Rondeau
Production #8731
Original air dates: 4/27/66 & 4/28/66

PLOT

Death in Slow Motion. The Riddler and his gang interrupt the silent film festival of a famous film collector Mr. Van Jones dressed as Charlie Chaplin and the Keystone Cops, long enough to entertain the moviegoers and steal the box office receipts. Batman and Robin trace the Riddler via a riddle to Mother Gotham's Bakery, where he plans to steal the company's payroll. The Riddler not only steals the payroll, but also films the entire robbery in the style of an old silent film comedy. The Dynamic Duo rush to the bakery, only to be greeted by another riddle from the already departed fiend.

This new riddle leads them to the Baker Street branch of the Gotham Library, where they are hit over the head by an oversized book—another sequence captured in its entirety by the Riddler's hidden camera. The riddles contained in the giant book lead them to a Temperance Party (where the only thing being served is lemonade) being given by Mr. Van Jones. As Robin waits outside in the Batmobile, Batman enters to find that the Riddler has spiked the lemonade with Temper Tonic, causing the good-natured party to turn into a hot-tempered free-for-all. Once again, the Riddler's ever-present camera catches the action.

Meanwhile, back at the Batmobile, the Riddler's new assistant, Pauline, dressed as Little Bo Peep, kidnaps the Boy Wonder and takes him to an abandoned lumberyard, where in a matter of moments a buzz saw will split him right down the middle.

The Riddler's False Notion. After leaving the party, Batman returns to the now empty Batmobile. There he finds more riddles, which lead him to the lumberyard, where the Riddler is filming Robin's demise under the teeth of a buzz saw. As Batman is poised to rescue Robin, the Riddler, dressed as a silent movie villain—complete with black hat, cape and moustache—attacks Batman with a bullwhip. Realizing the boy is in danger, Batman rushes to the saw, giving the Riddler and his men time to escape. When Batman reaches the boy, he finds he has been duped by a dummy dressed as Robin.

Just then, Pauline tries to make her escape but is quickly captured by Batman, who, along with Commissioner Gordon, returns to the Batcave. There Pauline reveals two riddles, which lead Batman to the top of the Chessman Building. Again, Batman finds the Riddler filming Robin, this time as the Boy Wonder is about to be pushed off a ledge to the street below. Batman throws a Batrope just as the Riddler shoves Robin off the ledge, and the boy catches it between his teeth. Batman then lifts him back to the ledge as the criminals make their escape in a helicopter, leaving a skywritten riddle in their wake.

This new riddle leads Batman and Robin to the home of Mr. Van Jones, who we learn had commissioned the Riddler to make a silent film comedy starring Batman in return for $100,000. Not content with the money, the Riddler decides to steal all of Mr. Van Jone's priceless silent film collection and hold it for ransom. The Caped Crusaders arrive in time to rescue Van Jones and his collection from the grip of the Riddler and his gang.

Writer Rik Vollaerts

"It was very hard to make a presentation there [to the producers], because they didn't really know what they were going to do. There were people involved that didn't know what it meant when you said, 'tongue-in-cheek.' There were people there that didn't know what the word *camp* meant. But there was a sufficient number of intelligent writers who saw what they had. You'll find a lot of variations. You will find some that took themselves seriously and some that didn't. The only thing that I did that was even partially different was to develop an intelligent supercriminal. I had a hell of a hard time trying to sell it because the number of people who read books in Hollywood is rather limited.

"The series was interesting because it was funny. Even the comic books were never intended to be serious.

"The only surprise I had in the series at all was the inability to do good special effects. By that I mean constructing artifacts that really do things."

BatFacts

- This episode marked one of the last performances by former silent screen star Francis X. Bushman. Coincidentally, Neil Hamilton (Commissioner Gordon) was also a silent screen star.
- This episode was based on a July 1965 *Batman* comic book story featuring the Joker, entitled "The Joker's Comedy Capers."

Special BatEquipment

Batkey
Bat Terror Control
Batscanner Receiver

Trivia Quiz 16

a. What did the Riddler use to open the safe in the bakery?

b. Whose birthday was celebrated in this two-part episode?

Guest Cast

Penguin—Burgess Meredith
Finella—Julie Gregg
Octopus—Victor Lundin
Shark—Dal Jenkins
Swordfish—Louie Elias
Millionaire—Frank Wilcox
Miss Natural Resources—Lisa Mitchell
Manager—Charles La Torre
Beauty—Ann Reece
Multimillionaire—Bill Williams

Teleplay & story by Sheldon Stark
Directed by Tom Gries
Production #8733
Original air dates: 5/4/66 & 5/5/66

Plot

Fine Finny Fiends. The Penguin kidnaps Alfred after luring him to a phony fish store selling cut-rate caviar. Alfred is then brainwashed by the conniving bird in preparation for the Penguin's plan to rob the Multimillionaires' Annual Award Dinner. Since Alfred is arranging the dinner, he is one of the few people who will know the secret location of the dinner and which bathing beauty will be chosen to accept the award money for this year's honored charity.

Before he can be missed, Alfred is returned home without the slightest idea of what happened to him, but Batman and Robin are perplexed by the very noticeable facial twitch he has developed. Later that day, a fish hook that has fallen out of Alfred's morning coat appears inside one of the canapes the butler prepared for the buffet before the awards. The hook tips off

Batman that the Penguin's hideout is on a fishing pier owned by the bird under the pseudonym Knott A. Fish.

The Penguin and his Finks capture the duo and place them inside a vacuum tank filled with balloons. As the air is slowly sucked out of the room, the balloons begin to break. When the last balloon has burst, Batman and Robin will be dead.

Batman Makes the Scenes. Believing the Dynamic Duo are dead, the Penguin and his men quickly rush off to establish their alibis. Meanwhile, Batman has reached the emergency tank of Batoxygen in his utility belt to stay conscious and uses his Batknife to cut the pair free of their bonds so they can escape the vacuum tank.

Now aware that Alfred has been brainwashed, Batman gives him the information the Penguin wants. When the Penguin calls Wayne Manor and signals Alfred to relay the information, the butler reveals that the dinner is to be held on board the S.S. *Gotham Neptune* and that the chosen beauty queen is Miss Natural Resources. The Penguin then releases Alfred from his power, causing the Butler to forget the whole conversation.

That night, Penguin switches his latest assistant, Finella, for Miss Natural Resources and arms her with an umbrella filled with knockout gas. Fearing for the safety of the attending millionaires, Bruce and Dick decide to attend the dinner as Batman and Robin. All goes well until it is time for the dessert, the giant cake containing Finella. As she pops from the cake, Finella gasses the millionaires with the umbrella. While everyone is unconscious, Penguin and his men scoop up all of the money intended for charity and rush back to their hideout to divide up the loot. Unknown to Penguin, Batman and Robin had taken Anti-Penguin-Gas Pills prior to the party and they were able to rush via a short-cut to the bird's hideout, where they lay in wait for the Penguin. After a good thrashing, Batman and Robin escort the villains back to prison.

BAT TALK
Actor Alan Napier

"I remember one time when Alfred was walking down the street to buy caviar for the millionaires' party. On the fish shop set was this big barrel of caviar covered with an umbrella. I was supposed to be tasting the caviar when the umbrella closed in on me, forcing my face into the barrel. That was most unpleasant, because the "caviar" was really black currant jam."

BATFACTS

- During the course of this two-part episode, Batman shows Alfred a series of criminal photographs in the hopes of jogging his memory. The first two photos he is shown are those of William Dozier and Howie Horwitz.

SPECIAL BATEQUIPMENT

Emergency Tank of Batoxygen
Batknife
Anti-Penguin-Gas Pills
Memory Batbank

TRIVIA QUIZ 17

Where does Alfred normally get his caviar?

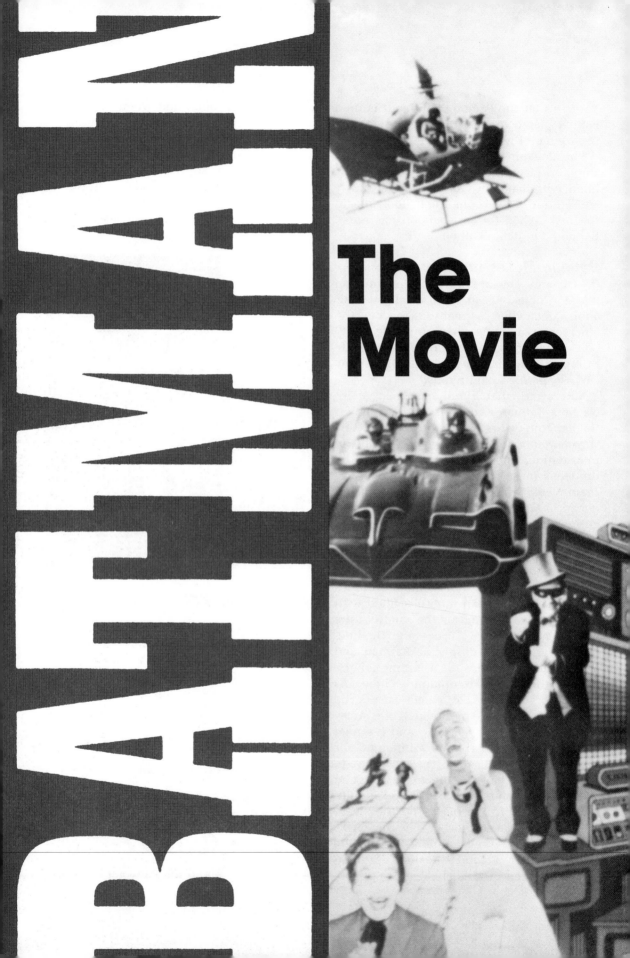

CAST

Catwoman (Kitka)—Lee Meriwether
Joker—Cesar Romero
Penguin—Burgess Meredith
Riddler—Frank Gorshin
Commodore Schmidlapp—Reginald Denny
Vice Admiral Fangschleister—Milton Frome
Quetch—George Sawaya
Morgan—Dick Crockett
Bluebeard—Gil Perkins
British Delegate—Maurice Dallimore
Japanese Delegate—Teru Shimada
West German Delegate—Ivan Triesault
Cameo (Rooftop)—Jack La Lanne

Screenplay & Story by Lorenzo Semple, Jr.
Directed by Leslie H. Martinson
Production #108
Original release date: 8/3/66

Acknowledgment*

We wish to express our gratitude to the enemies of crime and crusaders against crime throughout the world for their inspirational example. To them and to lovers of adventure, lovers of pure escapism, lovers of unadulterated entertainment, lovers of the ridiculous and the bizarre . . . to fun lovers everywhere this picture is respectfully dedicated.

If we have overlooked any sizable group of lovers, we apologize.

—The Producers

The Batman movie was originally scheduled to be made prior to the television series. However, when ABC found that many of its television shows were failing, they ordered the Batman series moved back from its fall, 1966 planned airdate to the midseason premiere of January 1966. The film which was intended to introduce the viewing public to the Batman characters, was put on hold until filming was completed on the first season of the series.

Since the series was such a success, one might wonder why ABC proceeded with the motion picture. Well, apart from the obvious financial incentives, the film served two functions. First, it was intended to aid the studio in selling the series to overseas markets. Secondly its larger budget allowed the producers to create the Batcopter and Batboat under the movie budget, and then use these impressive vehicles in the series. As the television budget was rather limited, the creation of the above mentioned items was beyond the financial limits of the series. In fact, the footage of the Batboat and Batcopter which was used in the series was lifted directly from the film and edited into the episodes where needed.

The Batcycle, which was also intended for the film, made its debut in the series ("The Penguin Goes Straight/Not Yet He Ain't") because it happened to be completed before filming had ended on the series.

*Shown at the beginning of the movie

Batman

PLOT

Acting on an anonymous warning that Commodore Schmidlapp is in danger, Bruce Wayne and Dick Grayson race back to Wayne Manor and, after donning their costumes, drive the Batmobile to the airport, where they board the Batcopter and fly off in search of the commodore's yacht.

Upon locating the yacht, Batman lowers the Batladder and prepares to board her, but just as he is about to set foot on the deck, the entire ship disappears. As Batman slowly sinks into the ocean, Robin raises the Batcopter and discovers that a huge shark has clamped its jaws around Batman's leg. While beating on the shark, Batman tells Robin over his Batradio to send down the can of Shark-Repellent Batspray. After turning on the auto pilot, Robin descends the ladder with the spray can and hands it to Batman. In a matter of moments, the spray does its work and the shark releases Batman and falls to the water below, only to explode on impact.

Hours later, in Commissioner Gordon's office, Batman and Robin find themselves on the receiving end of a thousand questions when a press conference is called to explain the ship's disappearance. Among the reporters is a certain Miss Kitka, a Russian reporter from the *Moscow Bugle*, who is really Catwoman in disguise. After the reporters leave, Batman, Robin, Gordon, and Chief O'Hara check the status of Gotham City's arch criminals and discover that Penguin, Joker, Riddler, and Catwoman have all been released from jail. Believing any of them could be responsible for the ship's disappearance, Batman and Robin race back to the Batcave to check on a vital clue.

Meanwhile, Miss Kitka returns to her waterfront hideout at Ye Olde Benbow Taverne, where she rejoins her villainous partners in crime. Catwoman changes back to her regular clothes and confronts her partners with the news of Batman's escape from the ex-

ploding shark trap. After checking on the captive commodore, the four members of the United Underworld fight among themselves until Penguin, realizing the Dynamic Duo by now will have figured out how the ship disappeared, plans another trap. He then has his submarine prepared for an immediate departure.

Back in the Batcave, Batman and Robin examine the film taken by the Automatic Batcopter Batcamera under a magnifying lens and discover an illegal marker buoy stationed at exactly the spot where the ship disappeared. Believing the criminals may have left fingerprints on the buoy, they drive the Batmobile to a secluded pier, switch to the Batboat and speed off in search of the criminal buoy.

Once they reach the buoy, they discover that a giant projector was used to project the image of the ship, but before they can examine it for fingerprints, Penguin who has been spying on the duo via the periscope in his Penguin Sub, turns on the super-powered magnet hidden in the buoy. The magnet attracts the metal objects in the duo's utility belts, pinning our heroes to the buoy. Penguin then orders Joker to fire torpedoes at them. Before the first two can reach them, Batman blows them up with the high-frequency signals from his Batradio. As the third torpedo speeds toward the buoy, the batteries in the radio give out. The villains hearing the subsequent explosion

and, seeing the buoy deserted, believe the duo have been destroyed. But thanks to a passing porpoise that intercepted the torpedo, the duo are very much alive.

Returning to the Batmobile, Batman phones the Pentagon and to his surprise finds that the Penguin purchased a war surplus preatomic submarine from the Navy. As the duo ponder the ramifications of this news the Riddler launches a Polaris missile from the sub, which subsequently skywrites two riddles that prove beyond the shadow of a doubt that the four villains are working together.

Back at the hideout, the villains discuss their plan to kidnap the members of the United World Security Council. Realizing they must first rid themselves of Batman and Robin they plan to kidnap Bruce Wayne. Batman will try to rescue Wayne, they assume, so they set a trap for the Dynamic Duo at their headquarters.

Catwoman, in the guise of Miss Kitka, pays a visit to Wayne Manor and shows Bruce a pair of riddles written on Wayne Foundation stationery, which were delivered to her apartment. Believing the riddles are a threat to Miss Kitka's life, Bruce arranges to spend the evening with her, while Robin and Alfred follow close behind in the Batmobile. After dinner and a carriage ride in the park (where Kitka secretly signals her partners that Bruce has fallen into the trap by accepting her invitation to visit her apart-

ment), Bruce escorts Kitka home. Meanwhile Penguin, Joker, Riddler, and their men fly to Kitka's apartment on jet-pack umbrellas. Arriving at the apartment, Bruce and Kitka are surprised by the villains. Although Bruce puts up a good fight, he is soon overpowered and quickly finds himself mounted on a jet pack umbrella, heading for the waterfront hideout. Robin who turned off the Micro-TV Batscanner during a romantic moment between Bruce and Kitka, spots the flying umbrellas with their human cargo and, having no alternative, returns to the Batcave.

As Joker puts the finishing touches on his trick jack-in-the-box, which the fiends hope will spring Batman into the waiting arms of the Penguin's exploding octopus, Bruce regains consciousness and demands to see Miss Kitka. Blindfolded and bound, Bruce is led to a room where Catwoman is waiting in the guise of Kitka. Bruce knows the three villains are listening via a hidden microphone, so he pretends that he has a secret transmitter hidden up his sleeve. As Kitka, who is also bound, tries to find the transmitter, the villains reappear. Returning to the main room with Batman, they untie his hands and attempt to remove the transmitter. But once Bruce is free of his bonds, he trounces the villains. During the fight, one of Penguin's men accidently falls on the trick jack-in-the-box and is immediately catapulted up and out of the window and into

the arms of the exploding octopus. Bruce subdues the villains long enough to reach the window and makes his escape by diving into the water below.

While Bruce returns to Wayne Manor, the villains proceed with their master plan. After transferring the commodore to the sub, Penguin uses the commodore's invention, the Total Dehydrator, to transform five of his men into small piles of colored dust. Placing them in separate vials, he plans to set another trap for Batman.

Having changed back to Batman, Bruce returns with Robin to Ye Olde Benbow Taverne, where he finds no sign of Miss Kitka or the villains, but instead finds a smoking bomb. Realizing the bomb could detonate any moment, Batman grabs it and runs off in search of a safe place to dispose of it. Batman disposes of the bomb in the nick of time. After being joined by Robin, the duo are surprised by the appearance of the Penguin disguised as Commodore Schmidlapp. The Penguin tricks them into returning with him to the Batcave, where he uses the drinking water dispenser to rehydrate his five henchmen.

Unfortunately, during the rehydrating process, Penguin unknowingly rehydrates his men with the heavy water used to recharge the atomic pile, causing them to become unstable. The five men soon revert to antimatter and disappear after their bodies receive the slightest impact. After putting the Penguin to sleep (for the second time) the duo drive him back to the city. However, along the way the Batmobile develops mechanical problems, and while Batman and Robin leave the car to find the trouble, Penguin gasses both of them and makes his getaway in the Batmobile. Moments later, the duo, having taken Anti-Penguin-Gas pills, pick themselves up and head for the Batcycle, which is cleverly hidden in the nearby bushes. Mounting the cycle, they proceed once again to the airport and, using the Batcopter, track the stolen Batmobile to the United World Building. However their flight is cut short when the Batcopter is hit by one of the Riddler's deadly skywriting missiles.

Just as it seems hopeless, the Batcopter crash-lands on the display pile of foam rubber set up outside the Foam Rubber Wholesaler's Convention. Realizing the security council is in danger, the Caped Crusaders run the remaining mile to the building. Meanwhile, Riddler, Joker, and Catwoman hae successfully navigated the sub through a narrow channel and arrived at the abandoned submarine dock underneath the building. Using the service elevator, they join Penguin and, with the help of the Total Dehydrator, make off with the entire security council in dehydrated form. Batman and Robin arrive just as the villains are making their escape. Threatening to kill Miss Kitka, Catwoman delays the duo long enough for the dastardly group to make their escpe in the service elevator. Remembering the submarine dock beneath the building, Batman deduces that the villains will try to make their escape out to sea via Short Island Sound.

Racing to the Batboat, the duo hope to be able to catch the sub before it is too late. As the villains gloat over their accomplishments and prepare to issue their ransom demands, Batman and Robin locate the sub. Penguin, having been alerted to the duo's arrival via sonar, orders the Riddler to launch a homing missile. As the missile homes in on our heroes, Batman gives Robin the missile's frequency and, using the Batra-dio, jams the missile so that it explodes harmlessly in the water.

Having failed with the missile, Penguin fires several torpedoes at the duo, but Robin destroys the deadly fish with Batcharges. As the sub tries to escape, Robin fires several additional rounds of Batcharges and drives the sub to the surface.

The Dynamic Duo board the sub and, after a fierce battle, round up the entire gang except Catwoman. As Batman attempts to handcuff the feline felon, she climbs up the conning tower and reenters the sub, and as she races through the control room, she trips and knocks off her mask. Batman and Robin, who followed her inside, are startled by the sudden realization that Catwoman and Kitka are one and the same person. As Robin handcuffs Catwoman, Batman radios the Coast Guard to collect the villains. Suddenly, Batman spots the rack of dehydrated council members, who survived the battle unscathed, perched at the edge of the plotting table. As Batman picks up the rack, Commodore Schmidlapp, who had been asleep during the battle, enters the control room, approaches Batman, trips, falls, and smashes the rack of dehydrated council members on the plotting table. To make matters worse, he sneezes and scatters the dust all over the place.

Having collected all of the dust, Batman returns to the Batcave, where he will try to separate the dust mixture with a Super-Molecular Dust Separator. After a successful separation, the duo transfer the dust to the United World Building, where they will attempt to rehydrate the council members. They hook up the necessary apparatus and Robin turns on the water faucet to restore the nine council members to their original form. Moments later the entire council reappears, and all seems well. On closer examination, however, we discover that the council members are not speaking their native languages. Realizing their work is finished (they believe this mixing of minds might aid world peace), the Dynamic Duo leave through the window to begin another adventure.

BATFACTS

- In the first draft of the shooting script, the jet-pack umbrellas (which originated in a February 1965 *Batman* comic book story) were supposed to be worn on the villains backs instead of being ridden.
- Also, the umbrellas were supposed to attract the attention of the Air Force, which, under the command of Colonel Terry, chases the villains in jet planes.
- The part of Colonel Terry, though never filmed, was listed in the film's press-book as being played by Sterling Holloway.
- Commodore Schmidlapp was originally clled Commodore Redhead.
- The first draft script called for the Penguin's exploding octopus to be a giant exploding umbrella.

BATEQUIPMENT

Instant Costume Change Lever
Batdrift Angle
Batladder
Automatic Bathold
Automatic Batcopter Bat Camera
Oceanic Repellent Batsprays:
Shark-repellent Batspray
Manta-Ray-repellent Batspray
Barracuda-repellent Batspray
Whale-repellent Batspray
Batradio
Magnifying Lens
Film Development Tank Super-Fine Batgrain
Navigational Aid Computer
Utility Belt Transmitter
Micro-TV Batscanner
Compressed Steam Batlift
Lunar Scanning Screen
Mobile Anticrime File
Batcamera's Polarized Batfilter
Super Blinding Batpellets
Anticrime Eye Pattern Master File
Drinking Water Dispenser
Anti-Penguin-Gas Pills
Batcycle Go Cart
Batcharge Launcher
Chemical Research Materials
Batcentrifuge
Super-Molecular Dust Separator

TRIVIA QUIZ 18

a. What was the name of Catwoman's pet cat?

b. What was the name of the restaurant Bruce Wayne took Miss Kitka to?

c. What name did the Penguin use to purchase the submarine?

d. Where was Miss Kitka's apartment located?

e. The rubber shark that attacked Batman appeared in another Fox film five years earlier. Can you name the film and whose pet it was in that film?

f. What is the wavelength frequency for the Riddler's Polaris missile?

BEHIND THE SCENES

As many of those involved with the movie recollect, making this movie was generally a joy and only sometimes a nightmare. Generally camaradery ruled, and creativity was evident everywhere. There were occasional mishaps and flareups, as in all huge endeavors of this nature.

During several interviews for this book, people mentioned Burt Ward's apparent difficulty in adjusting to the series' overnight success. Producer **William Dozier**'s only bad experience of this nature occured during the making of the movie, as he comments:

"The only time I had a little problem with Burt, and that wasn't much, was when he would talk about his 'million-dollar face.' During those explosions that we would have on the sets, sometimes as part of those special effects, he would become worried about his 'million-dollar face,' and he was serious. One day when we were shooting the feature, I went over on the set, and they

were sitting around. I said, 'What's the matter?' and they said, 'Burt is not here. He is over in the infirmary.' I said, 'What's the matter with him?' They said he had some sort of problem. So, I went over to the infirmary on the lot and said, 'What is the matter with you?' Well, he said, 'I have this pain.' I said, 'While you are enjoying that pain, get your ass over to the set.' He said 'Yes, sir,' and went back on the set immediately. But that was the way you had to treat him. He was an absolute baby.''

Dozier recalled a far more serious incident, occuring near the time of the movie's premiere:

"The Batboat was quite a thing. It was build by the Glastron boat company in Austin, Texas. That is why we premiered the movie in Austin, Texas. The premiere was on Saturday and Monday was when that guy started shooting off the Tower in Austin, Texas, and killed about forty or fifty people.

AT THE BATMAN MOVIE

On Saturday, we all rode in an open car down the main street, but he was only interested in killing students, thank heaven.''

A risky premiere and temperamental actors were not the only problems which arose as director **Leslie H. Martinson** elaborates:

"The one mishap was the fight on the submarine, with all of the men dueling up there, and it was in the tank on the back lot that Fox had out in the valley. Apparently, stuntman Ace Hudkins lost his footing and slipped off the side of the submarine and hit his head on the bottom, which was only about three and a half feet deep. He cracked his head open and knocked himself unconscious. I called 'Cut,' and the cameras stopped (there were three cameras going), and suddenly someone said, 'Where is Ace?' Just like that, the stuntmen just all disappeared underwater. They dragged him up and rushed him to the hospital. You could just wonder how he survived that tremendous laceration on the top of his head. A friend of mine—a very, very close friend who was a top neurosurgeon and was then chief of staff—happened to be at the hospital and attended Ace, and he eventually recovered.''

Of course, these incidents were exceptional, and the overall result was a hit worldwide. Martinson continues:

"I will never forget a walk I took from Curzon Street to Upper Grosvenor, which is about six blocks in London. I was there doing a film, another film for Fox immediately following the *Batman* film, called *Fathom*. It was Raquel Welch's first big film. I met Adam at the White Elephant, which is a restaurant on Curzon; sort of a show business restaurant. Adam and I had lunch, and then we had this short walk, and he was just absolutely mobbed. He stepped out onto the sidewalk, and someone recognized him, and from then on it was just sheer bedlam, with hundreds of English people following us.''

Julie Newmar was originally cast to play the Catwoman in the film. She was, however, unavailable when the time came to shoot the film, so the part had to be recast. Lee Meriwether recalls how she got the part:

"I had to read for the part, and there were five girls in the outer office when I got there to read. They gave me a scene, and I went into the office, and I thought, I really have to do something to make them remember me as those other girls were really gorgeous, so I decided I would do things like a cat. So, I curled myself up in the chair, and I licked my hand like a paw and did a little preening and purring and things like that. Luckily, I had a lot of cats, and in one of my lives I was a cat. I remember Les Martinson said to them, 'I didn't tell her to do that.' So, it all kind of worked, and I had the part. To show you how far down to the wire they were, they were already filming while I was reading, because I went in for costumes and they shot around the character in the submarine. My first day was working in the submarine with a lot of things going wrong and steam coming out.''

Having won the role of the Catwoman, Lee now had to face up to working with her three villainous co-stars (all of whom, by this time, were quite comfortable in their roles). Lee recalls her first meeting with the trio:

"Cesar was the one who took me under his wing when I came on the set. He welcomed me, and he said, 'Don't worry, you'll do fine. Let me help you, and if there is anything I could do to help you, just let me know.' So, in the actual filming, he would position me into place, because I was wearing a mask. My field of vision was almost tunnel. So, I missed my mark a couple of times, and he just eased me and pushed me right to the place where we were supposed to end up. He was right there and always wonderful.

"Frank [Gorshin] was the most subdued of all the gentlemen, although Burgess [Meredith] was quiet, but Burgess and I hit it off and talked for hours and went to the movies together while we were on location in Santa Barbara. We went for two days' location on the Santa Barbara pier. I remember Frank being very particular about his costume, and he had a suit that had been made for him, a special suit. He wanted to wear it in the movie, because he was tired of wearing the green tights. I remember the jacket was smashing; it really was, even though it was garish. It looked good on him.

"Both Burgess and I got to play dual characters in the movie, which was fun. Kitanya Irenya Tatanya Kerenska Alisoff—I had to learn that name in five minutes, before I had to film it. It was a delightful experience working with these pros.

"Burgess gave the girls, my two daughters Kyle and Lesley, one of the rubberized plastic noses. I really made it in the girls' eyes when I became Catwoman. I had to do 'Star Trek' or 'Batman.' I did both, but if I hadn't done 'Batman,' I would have been nothing."

Although stunt people were used during the making of the film most of the time, the actors occasionally did their own stunts. Lee Meriwether remembers the stunts she was asked to perform:

"During the submarine explosion scene, we fell over on each other; we did a lot of that stuff ourselves. The only time that they had a stuntwoman do a stunt for me, I think, is the one that does not look good in the show, wher I trip and fall and my mask falls off. I said, 'Why can't I do it? It is such a simple thing.' They said no and I said OK. I had been really worried about using the bullwhip on Hubie [Kearns, Adam West's stuntman]. I had to use a bullwhip to pull him back, when he was dressed as Adam and not Batman, and I missed him and hit his leg. It was terrible, and I said I wanted a stuntwoman for that because I was not doing a good job, I was so afraid of hurting him."

Stuntwork, however, was not the only thing the actors were allowed to do: improvisation was another. According to Lee Meriwether, Burgess Meredith add-libbed quite a bit during the scene involving the five dehydrated guinea pigs. While the meanies are pouring the powdery bodies of the men into separate vials, the lines about being careful as "each of them has a mother" are all Burgess' creation.

The actors were not the only ones who improvised on the set. Director **Leslie H. Martinson** recalls his creation of the infamous bomb sequence:

"I improvised the sequence where Batman tries to get rid of the bomb. I mean, it was one little thing, and I put in the thing with the ducks and the lovers and the other things. It was a good film."

ROGUES' GALLERY
(clockwise spiral from upper left corner)

Vincent Price (Egghead),

Shelley Winters (Ma Parker),

Julie Newmar (Catwoman),

Frank Gorshin (Riddler),

Otto Preminger (Mr. Freeze),

Tallulah Bankhead (Black Widow),

Anne Baxter (Zelda the Great),

Van Johnson
(Minstrel),
Burgess Meredith
(Penguin) and
Ethel Merman (Lola Lasagne),
Victor Buono (King Tut),
and Cesar Romero (Joker).

Two months after the film was completed production resumed on the series. With the addition of the previously mentioned new Bat-Equipment and several new villains (added to the list of returning foes) Batman began its second season. However, unlike its first season, the ratings which had once been overwhelming were bordering on average. It was only a few months since Batman's first appearance, but already the public was beginning to lose interest.

One way the producers tried to keep a hold on its audience was to add three-part adventures; another was by forming team-ups with several of the villains. It worked for the film version so why not try it in the series?

However, regardless of the various ways the producers tried to save the Caped Crusader, the ratings never climbed as high as they had begun.

As the second season drew to a close, the producers decided that a new character should be added to help raise Batman's sagging ratings. So Batgirl, who made her first comic book appearance in early 1967, entered the Batworld.

Prior to Batgirl's addition to the show a trial pilot film using Batgirl was produced. As actor **Joey Tata** explains:

"In the Pilot to 'Batgirl' (originally the test, because there was test for 'Batgirl'), Tim Herbert was playing the Killer Moth, in a green and yellow bug suit; that was the first time they were introducing Yvonne, but it was never used."

One of the difficulties in adding Batgirl to the show was selecting her costume—her mask actually changed over the course of the season. Everything about the show seems to have had its funny side, though, as Barrie Howard (daughter of the late producer **Howie Horwitz**) explains:

"I remember my father had to choose the color scheme for Batgirl's costume, and he had to try to match it to Batman's cape so it wouldn't clash. The funny part about it was that he was color-blind and couldn't tell one color from another."

A few other severe changes flew in with Batgirl. The time slot changed from twice weekly to once weekly (on Thursdays). This dramatically changed the shows themselves, for the producers felt the cliff-hanger endings would be difficult to remember from week to week. Instead, they opted for ending a storyline within a half hour, then introducing the next week's villain at the end of each week's show.

The character of Aunt Harriet was reduced to two cameo appearances during the third season. This was done to accommodate Madge Blake who was in ill health (she died on February 19, 1969), as well as for economic reasons. When the series was reduced from its regular twice a week airing to once a week, the scriptwriters were limited to a maximum of thirteen characters per episode. So, after Batman, Robin, Batgirl and their alter-egos of Bruce, Dick and Barbara (who each count as a separate character), Alfred, Chief O'Hara and Commissioner Gordon, there was only room for the villain and a couple of henchmen.

Second
Season

35—Shoot a Crooked Arrow
36—Walk the Straight & Narrow

Cast

Archer—Art Carney
Maid Marilyn—Barbara Nichols
Crier Tuck—Doodles Weaver
Big John—Loren Ewing
Alan A. Dale—Robert Cornthwaite
Everett Bannister—Archie Moore
1st Guard—Steve Pendleton
2nd Guard—Lee Delano
Cop—James O'Hara
Pedestrian—Myran Dell
Zoltan Zorba—Sam Jaffe
1st Poor Person—Robert Adler
2nd Poor Person—Heidi Jenson
3rd Poor Person—Kitty Kelly
Cameo (window)—Dick Clark

Teleplay & story by Stanley Ralph Ross
Directed by Sherman Marks
Production #9705
Original air dates: 9/7/66 & 9/8/66

Plot

Shoot a Crooked Arrow. The Archer and his band of merry criminals pay a surprise visit to Wayne Manor, where they gas everyone and then make off with the loose cash Bruce kept in the wall safe, distributing it to the poor people of Gotham City.

Later that day, the Archer attempts to flaunt justice by visiting Commissioner Gordon's office. After blinding everyone with another of his trick arrows, he proceeds to whack the Dynamic Duo in the knees before making his escape out the window.

As the Archer and his men distribute the money they recently stole from Everett Bannister's Koin Machines Inc., they are captured by Batman and Robin. However, they are quickly bailed out of jail by the city's poor people, who look upon them as their heroes.

Batman traces Archer to his hideout at the Earl Huntington Archery Range in the Green Forest section of the city, where Alfred attempts to distract the villain in an archery contest long enough for the duo to search his headquarters. Unfortunately, the duo set off a secret alarm and are subsequenty caught up in a giant net. After stringing our heroes up by their thumbs, Archer threatens

to behead Alfred unless Batman reveals the location of the Batcave (Archer plans to enter the Batcave and destroy the crime-predicting computers). Batman notices that the guillotine Archer plans to use on Alfred is a fake prop used by stage magicians and refuses to comply. Realizing his plan has failed, Archer moves our heroes outdoors, where, after tying them to a stake, he and his men (mounted on horseback) prepare to run them both through with lances.

Walk the Straight & Narrow. Just as the duo are about to be skewered, they activate the Batsprings concealed in their boots and catapult up and out of the way. Rather than try to recapture the duo, the Archer and his men decide to make a quick getaway to their new hideout in the basement of police headquarters.

Next, Archer and his men hijack the armored car containing the $10,000,000 the Wayne Foundation is planning to donate to the city's poor people. The truck is later found abandoned nearby with the money still intact, so the presentaion ceremony continues on schedule. While Alfred, dressed as Batman, watches from across the street, Bruce attends the ceremony, where it is discovered that Archer had replaced the money in the armored car with counterfeit money bearing the face of the Archer.

Batman deduces that Alan A. Dale, one of the directors of the Wayne Foundation, who was responsible for the delivery of the money, is a member of Archer's gang and that they are planning to escape by boat to Switzerland. Batman and Robin head to the Batboat and intercept and capture Archer and his men before they reach international waters.

BatTalk
Writer Stanley Ralph Ross

"You had to tell Art [Carney] who you want him to imitate. You say, 'I want you to imitate Cary Grant.' He will do what he thinks is Cary Grant, but no one else will know it's Cary Grant."

BatFacts

- The Archer escaped from police headquarters in a moving van from the Trojan Hearse Company, driven by Maid Marilyn.
- The character of Zoltan Zorba was originally known as Alan A. Aardvark, but when it was decided that Sam Jaffe was going to play the part it was changed to Zorba as sort of a parody on his character, Dr. Zorba, on "Ben Casey."

Special BatEquipment

Batfile
Batsprings
Batpole Negate Bruce's [Costume] Change Switch
Batspeech Imitator
Batcrime Computer
Lunar Scanning Screen
Terrestrial Scanner

Trivia Quiz 19

a. What is Alfred's nickname, and what weapon is he an expert with?

b. How many arrows can you buy for one dollar at the Archer's Archery Range?

37—HOT OFF THE GRIDDLE
38—THE CAT AND THE FIDDLE

GUEST CAST

Catwoman—Julie Newmar
Jack O'Shea—Jack Kelly
John—Buck Kartalian
Charles—George Barrows
Thomas—Charles Horvath
Hostess—Edy Williams
Ralph Staphylococcus (Driver)—James Brolin
Cramer—George Neise
Zubin Zuccini—David Fresco

Teleplay and story by Stanley Ralph Ross
Directed by Don Weis
Production #9703
Original air dates: 9/14/66 & 9/15/66

PLOT

Hot Off the Griddle. Catwoman returns to open a school for cat burglars. Batman is tipped off to her presence after her Catmen steal a Catalogue, a Catamaran, and three little mittens, so he leaks a story to gossip columnist Jack O'Shea about a rare canary on display at the Natural History Museum, hoping Catwoman will pounce on the bird. Unknown to Batman, O'Shea is a member of Catwoman's gang. So, when the duo arrive at the museum, they are attacked by the cat burglars and shot by Catwoman with tranquilizer darts. She orders her men to throw the duo out the window, only to have them saved from certain death by the safety net they had installed, just in case the canary was dropped out the window.

They later trace the Catwoman to her lair at the Pink Sand Box nightclub where they are quickly deposited by a revolving booth into a room with a metal floor. The floor turns red hot—our heroes hop to it. Hoping to cool the floor, Batman breaks an overhead water pipe, only to find it contains Catatonic, a gas that knocks the duo unconscious.

They recover outside, strapped to a pair of aluminum reflectors, their bodies greased with margarine and two giant magnifying glasses poised over their hearts.

The Cat and the Fiddle. As luck would have it, a solar eclipse occurs just as the sun is about to fry the duo's hearts. Using their feet, they shift the magnifying glasses so that the sun will now burn off their bonds.

Back at the Batcave, Batman and Ro' in deduce Catwoman's next objective. The duo rush to the Gotham State Building and discover a momentous sale of Zubin Zuccini's two rare violins is to take place on the 102nd floor.

Meanwhile, Catwoman gasses rich recluse, Minerva Mathews, and takes her place as the purchaser of the violins.

The disguised Catwoman goes to the 102nd floor, disabling the elevators behind her. She greedily tries to steal the two violins from Zuccini, only to find that he is actually Robin· in disguise. Meanwhile, Batman attaches the new Batjet to one of the stalled elevators. The thrust is just enough to send Batman and the elevator to the top floor.

Batman arrives in time to rescue the outnumbered Boy Wonder. After having disposed of her men, Batman finds Catwoman outside on the ledge (with the money and violins, of course). Batman secures one end of the batrope, tosses the frightened Catwoman the other end, and tells her to drop the (fake) violins and money, and tie the rope around her waist.

Suddenly, O'Shea recovers and shoves Batman out the window. Robin knocks O'Shea senseless and finds Batman has caught hold of the rope holding the Catwoman, and the two are now hanging onto each other for dear life. Robin single-handedly pulls the two to safety.

BatTalk

Actress Julie Newmar

"It was so wonderful being on that show, because you could be nasty and mean, and in the fifties women could never (unless you were some 'B' picture actress) be mean, bad, and nasty. It was so satisfying; I can't tell you how satisfying it was.

"I had, of all people to play opposite me, James Brolin, making his first appearance, I think it was, on the screen. Here he was, playing this delicious truck driver. I introduced him to his wife, too. She was working as a secretary for one of the production people, and they fell madly in love and have two sons.

"Playing the part of Minerva Mathews was one of the favorite parts of my whole career, because it wasn't something I could just walk on and do: put the lipstick on, sashay on, throw the hip out, and play the favorite calendar girl part that I had already played. Being old was quite a study, and I had time to do it, so I would go down and sit in MacArthur Park, and I would watched aged people try to get up from the benches and then sit down. I observed this strongly enough to get the feeling that when you are old what you are thinking about is being *young.* You don't try to play old when you are old; you try to be young. I also went to a dentist to see what he could do to distort my face; you need more than makeup on a young face to look old. So he gave me this cotton roll, which I put in my lower lip, which lowered the jaw so that it looked like the upper teeth were missing. Then I added the hair and the slight hump in the back, and when I came out of my dressing room, there were three fellas who came over to give me a chair to sit on. I didn't know if they knew who I was, but I sure felt comfortable sitting there, and I grabbed those young men. It was the first opportunity that I had to be aggressively sexy. By myself I can't be aggressive, but when I was old playing that part, I could be that aggressive old lady. I could just get those boys and put my hand right up their knee, and I could get away with it. Now nobody else could do that, so I had a great time doing that."

BatFacts

- We discover in this episode that Alfred suffers from a back injury obtained in the war. This was probably just an excuse made up to prevent his having to Catusi with Aunt Harriet.
- George Barrows is best known for portraying the title role in the film *Robot Monster* and for playing gorillas in various other movies.
- Buck Kartialian went on to portray the werewolf in the telvision series "The Monster Squad."
- James Brolin made the first of his three Batman appearances in this episode before moving on to costar on "Marcus Welby, M.D."

Special BatEquipment

Batindex
Batjets

Trivia Quiz 20

What was the name of the rock group that recorded the Catusi?

39—The Minstrel's Shakedown
40—Barbecued Batman

Guest Cast

Minstrel—Van Johnson
Amanda—Leslie Perkins
Treble—Norman Grabowski
Bass—Remo Pisani
Courtland—John Gallaudet
Putnam—Army Archerd
Policeman in Basement—James O'Hara
TV Newsman—Del Moore
Broker #1—Eddie Garrett
Broker #2—Herbert Moss
Broker #3—Stu Wilson
Waiter #1—Tom Anthony
Waiter #2—Vince Dedrick
Scrubwoman—Phyllis Diller

Teleplay & story by Francis & Marian Cockrell
Directed by Murray Golden
Production #9713
Original air dates: 9/21/66 & 9/22/66

Plot

The Minstrel's Shakedown. The Minstrel, a lute-playing electronics genius, sends the stock market into an uproar when he changes the computerized stock quotations. He later demands $1,000 a week from each exchange member, or he will continue to interfere with the stock quotations, eventually causing the stock market to crash.

Batman and Robin try to capture the musical fiend later that night when he attempts to readjust his criminal circuits, but Minstrel escapes after blinding them with one of his electrical gadgets.

Batman tries to track Minstrel to his hideout by tracing with the Batdrone plane the television broadcast signal Minstrel used to air his threats. But Minstrel predicts that Batman will attempt just that and decides to broadcast from his criminal studio at the Willow Street Warehouse rather than from his hideout, as he normally does. Batman and Robin locate the warehouse and while attempting to surprise the Minstrel are caught and tied to a giant electrical spit, which when activated will slowly roast them over an electronic radar grill.

Barbecued Batman. Just as it looks like the end for our heroes, the adhesive Bat-bombs Batman planted earlier begin to explode, distracting Minstrel and his men long enough for Batman to shake the spit loose from its supports, allowing them to free themselves. When the Minstrel realizes that Batman has escaped, he and his men head for their secret hideout, leaving his assistant Amanda behind. Batman secretly places a bugging device in her handbag before letting her go, in the hopes that she will lead them to Minstrel's hideout.

Surprised by Amanda's return, Minstrel locates the bug in her purse and informs the eavesdropping Batman that he will now proceed with plan "High C," and that Batman should gather the exchange members at the stock exchange building in 30 minutes for a demonstration of his plan.

Minstrel carries out his threat, causing the entire building to vibrate by broadcasting a signal that corresponds to the building's resonance. Minstrel restates his blackmail demands over the air and threatens further that, if they are not met, he will destroy the building within one hour.

Batman figures Minstrel will be unable to broadcast his destructive signal without power, so he has all the power in the building shut off. However, this does not stop Minstrel, who broadcasts his own power. Once again, Minstrel broadcasts his demands, but Batman realizes that the broadcast has been prerecorded when he sees through Minstrel's disguise as one of the members of the stock exchange. Minstrel and his men, who were disguised as caterers, are quickly captured by the Dynamic Duo.

BatTalk

Executive Producer William Dozier

"These people [actors] would call up, or they would send their agents around, saying, can't so and so be on? Gloria Swanson, I remember, called me from New York, but we couldn't find the right part for her. But everybody came out of the woodwork; we never had to go after those people. A lot of them I had known personally, and they would call and say that they would love to do one of those because 'my kids want me to do it.' I don't think anyone had more fun with it than 'Buzz' Meredith."

BatFacts

- The Minstrel did not take part in a Batfight as he detested physical violence.

Special BatEquipment

Batdrone Plane
Giant Lighted Lucite Map of Gotham City
Batdrone Control Retriever Switch
Adhesive Batbombs
Particle Batacceleration Units
Directional Beam

Trivia Quiz 21

Which mythologial animal did the Minstrel wear on his shirt?

41—THE SPELL OF TUT
42—TUT'S CASE IS SHUT

GUEST CAST

King Tut—Victor Buono
Cleo Patrick—Marianna Hill
Royal Lapidary—Peter Mamakos
Amenophis Tewfik—Michael Pataki
Sethos—Boyd Santell
Royal Apothecary—Sid Haig
Man of Distinction—Rene Paul
Cameo (window)—Van Williams & Bruce Lee
  (as Green Hornet & Kato)

Teleplay and story by Robert C. Dennis & Earl
  Barret
Directed by Larry Peerce
Production #9709
Original air dates: 9/28/66 & 9/29/66

PLOT

The Spell of Tut. Batman and Robin are
called in to investigate the theft of a string of
amber beads by a pair of Egyptian-garbed
felons from the home of a wealthy man.
Their only clue, a lead pestle left behind by
the thieves, leads them to the Apex Apothecary Shop, where they find King Tut trying
to revive the scarabs imprisoned in the
amber beads.

During a Batfight, the duo are momentarily waylaid by some sneezing powder,
giving Tut and his Tutlings time to escape
with the now revived scarabs. Batman and
Robin quickly recover and discover a lone
scarab left behind by the fleeing pharoah.

Returning to the Batcave with the bug,
they eventually discover that, armed with
the once extinct scarabs, Tut will be able to
produce enough *Abu raubu simbu tu*, an
ancient drug that paralyzes the will, to put
all of Gotham City under his power.

Batman decides to set a trap for the mis-
guided monarch. He has the sphinx Tut

used to make his ill-fated predictions (See
episodes 27 and 28) delivered to the front
lawn of Wayne Manor. Hoping that Tut's
men will steal the statue, he has Robin hide
inside it.

Tut takes the bait and retrieves his evil
property. While in contact with Batman,
Robin accidentally drops his Batcommunicator, alerting Tut of his presence. Robin is
then dragged from the statue and is about to
be made the guinea pig for Tut's evil drug
when he overpowers Tut's men and escapes
through an unlocked door. Hoping to reach
the outside, Robin instead finds himself on a
narrow platform suspended over a pit filled
with Tut's pet crocodiles. As Batman rushes
to the rescue, the platform is slowly pulled
out from under the Boy Wonder.

Tut's Case is Shut. Batman finds Tut's hideout by tracing the Radioactive Bat-pellets he planted in Robin's utility belt with the Batgeiger Counter in the Batmobile. Using the Batlaser, he burns away the bars guarding the window to the crocodile pit. Then he swings across the room on his Batrope and grabs Robin just as the platform disappears completely.

Returning to the Batmobile, Robin informs Batman that Commissioner Gordon's summer secretary, Cleo Patrick, is really Tut's new Queen of the Nile. Intent on warning Gordon of the danger, Batman calls the office but gets Chief O'Hara. Unfortunately, the warning comes too late; O'Hara has already been given Tut's paralyzing drug in the form of a vitamin pill. As Batman and Robin rush back to the city, Tut appears at the office and on a whim has O'Hara perform acrobatics outside on the ledge. While watching O'Hara perform, Tut spots the Batmobile pull up to the building and quickly makes a hasty retreat as the Dynamic Duo arrive to rescue O'Hara from the ledge.

Later, Gordon (now also under Tut's spell) meets Batman in the park and drugs his lemonade. Now apparently under Tut's spell, Batman is led away with Robin by Tut's men to his hideout. As Tut prepares to leave for the waterworks to spike the city's water supply with his drug, Batman (who had wisely protected himself from the drug by coating his stomach with buttermilk) snaps out of his fake trance, and he and Robin trounce Tut's men.

Tut runs outside to the truck containing his deadly drug. Fortunately, Tut is unable to get the truck started, giving the Caped Crusaders time to finish off the Tutlings and race outside to release the contents of the truck into the gutter. Tut tries to prevent the flow of bug juice and accidentally swallows some of it, turning himself into Batman's slave. Later, in Gordon's office, Tut reverts once again to his real personality.

BATFACTS

- The Green Hornet and Kato appear at the window as Batman and Robin climb up the wall. The duo recognize the Hornet and Kato and identify them as crimefighters, yet in a later episode they will be thought of as criminals.
- Stafford Repp died on November 5, 1974.

SPECIAL BATEQUIPMENT

Batscope
BatRadio
Batgeiger Counter
Miniature Model of the Batgeiger Counter
Radioactive Batpellets
Batray Gun

TRIVIA QUIZ 22

a. How many gallons of bug juice did the Royal Apothecary say he could make?

b. Whose wedding anniversary takes place in this episode?

43—The Greatest Mother of Them All
44—Ma Parker

Guest Cast

Ma Parker—Shelley Winters
Legs—Tisha Sterling
Mad Dog—Michael Vandever
Pretty Boy—Robert Biheller
Machine Gun—Peter Brooks
Warden Crichton—David Lewis
Tiger—James Griffith
Chairlady—Fran Ryan
Prison Guard—Budd Perkins
Lefty (cameo)—Milton Berle
Catwoman (cameo)—Julie Newmar

Teleplay & story by Henry Slesar
Directed by Oscar Rudolph
Production #9707
Original air dates: 10/5/66 & 10/6/66

Plot

The Greatest Mother of Them All.

Gangster Ma Parker and her family—Pretty Boy, Mad Dog, Machine Gun, and Legs—invade Gotham City. They first appear at the Ladies Auxiliary's Mother of the Year Awards and rob the entire audience.

Batman and Robin are called into action. They quickly locate Ma and her brood at their home on Cherry Blossom Road, where under the cover of a smoke bomb they avoid capture, with the exception of Pretty Boy. Machine Gun, too, is captured later, after the family robs a theater box office. Then Mad Dog is caught, a holdup at a drugstore. They finally trace Ma and Legs to an old folks' home, where Ma tries to escape in a rocket-powered wheelchair but is stopped by a well-placed wall. Batman and Robin quickly transport the two women to the state pen to join the rest of their family.

As the Duo depart the prison, they notice a trustee examining the Batmobile's engine. Shrugging off his suspicious behavior as curiosity, they depart. Back in the warden's office, Ma reveals that she has secretly been replacing all of the warden's staff with her "boys." She also boasts that Batman was helping her when he captured her family, because now she has total control of the prison. Unknown to Batman, the curious trustee planted a bomb inside the Batmobile, which is set to explode when the Batmobile reaches 60 mph.

Ma Parker.

As the Dynamic Duo speed back to the Batcave, Batman becomes suspicious of a comment the trustee made regarding the speed of the Batmobile and immediately stops the car. He removes the bomb just as it was about to explode. They immediately return to the prison to check on the Parker family. Everything seems normal, so they leave once again. Ma then holds a meeting of the prison inmates, informing them of her plan to use the prison as a hideout while they commit their crimes. After all, who would look for escaped criminals inside a prison?

During an armored car robbery, Ma dy-

namites the truck, and the subsequent explosion sets off the Batseismograph, alerting Batman and Robin. The Caped Crusaders rush to the scene, where under a shower of money Ma and her gang make their escape—but not before Batman tears off a sleeve from one of the criminals' shirts. Upon closer examination, they discover it to be made of the same material used for prison clothing. Suspecting Ma Parker is somehow involved, they sneak into the prison and are quickly captured and strapped to a pair of electric chairs, scheduled to be fried at midnight.

Tricking Legs into leaving the room, Batman breaks off one of the elecrical wires and uses it to signal Alfred back in the Batcave. Midnight arrives, and Ma returns to pull the switch. Just as the switch is thrown, the power shuts off. The message Batman gave Alfred was to have the power company turn off the electricity at exactly midnight. Our heroes quickly free themselves and recapture Ma and her family.

BatTalk

Executive Producer William Dozier

"We turned the design for the Batmobile over to George Barris, who built it. We stupidly didn't buy it; we paid him so much per episode for it. Then he made two or three more and rented them around the country and still does, I'm told. But then when we did 'Green Hornet,' we thought we were a little smarter. We paid him to build the Black Beauty, but we bought it, so it was ours. We had two of those, and when the show was over, I discovered that Fox was going to sell it. I said, 'Wait a minute. Fox doesn't own it, entirely.' I remember my company got five thousand dollars from the sale. I don't know whom he sold it to.

"The Batmobile had a 1951 Chrysler chassis, and it wouldn't go over forty miles an hour. We would undercrank it to make it look like it would go about eighty."

BatFacts

- Although the bomb was set to go off when the Batmobile reached 60 mph, the car couldn't travel faster than 40 mph.

Batman was nominated for an Emmy in 1966 in the category of Outstanding Comedy Series.

Special BatEquipment

Batcrime Computer
Batseismograph
Hyperspectrographic Analyzer
Emergency Batturn Lever
Transistor Short-Wave Radio
Bat Receiver

Trivia Quiz 23

What film was playing at the movie theater that Ma Parker robbed?

45—THE CLOCK KING'S CRAZY CRIMES
46—THE KING GETS CROWNED

GUEST CAST

Clock King—Walter Slezak
Second Hand Three—Michael Pate
Millie Second—Eileen O'Neill
Benson Parkhurst—Ivan Triesault
Harry Hummert—Herbert Anderson
Mrs. Frontenac—Louise Lorimer
Fred Forbes—Jerry Doggett
Car Hop—Linda Lorimer
Boy—Roger Bacon
Girl—Sandra Lynn
Cameo (Window)—Sammy Davis, Jr.

Teleplay & story by Bill Finger & Charles
 Sinclair
Directed by James Neilson
Production #9711
Original air dates: 10/12/66 & 10/13/66

PLOT

The Clock King's Crazy Crimes. The master of time crimes, Clock King, arranges for one of his trick clocks to be sold to Harry Hummert Jewelry Shop, which caters to the rich people of Gotham City. Concealed inside the clock is a small TV camera that allows Clock King to observe everyone in the shop. Alerting his men, the Second Hands, he activates the tricky mechanism in the clock, releasing knockout gas. As soon as everyone is unconscious, the Second Hands arrive and pick the place clean.

Alerted to the robbery by Commissioner Gordon, the duo rush to Hummert's shop, where they learn that the clock was purchased at the Parkhurst Gallery. They quickly leave the shop and head for the gallery, where they discover that the clock was put up for auction by a Mr. Kronos. Deducing that it was Clock King in disguise, the duo head for Dunbar's Drive-in in search of Thelma Thymepiece, one of Clock King's former assistants.

Meanwhile, back at the Parkhurst Gallery, Clock King, in the guise of Progress Pigment, a pop art expert, attempts to steal a rare time-related painting under the very noses of the television audience (the local TV news was doing a live remote from the gallery when Clock King arrived). After making a short speech to the attending crowd, Clock King unveils his latest creation, called *Time Out of Joint*, which resembles the insides of a giant clock and when activated gives off a variety of different sounds and noises as the mechanical parts move about. No one is aware that the mechanical marvel is actually being used as a decoy to cover up the sound of a saber saw (attached to the rear of the sculpture) cutting through the wall into the strong room filled with valuable paintings.

After the saw has done its work, Clock King activates another switch on the sculpture, releasing a high-pitched sound that knocks everyone unconscious except him and his men, who were wearing earmuffs. Clock King enters the strong room and removes the clock masterpiece. Just as he is about to depart, Batman and Robin, who have been watching Clock King on the Batscope in the Batmobile, appear. After clobbering the Second Hands, the duo are stopped by the Clock King, who releases a barrage of giant springs at them from a hidden compartment in the sculpture. While the duo try to pry themselves free of the coils of time, the Clock King and his men make their escape.

Batman and Robin trace Clock King to his hideout at the Tick Tock Synthetic Rubies, Inc., factory, via the dust found inside one of

the Clock King's wristwatches left behind at the gallery. Unaware that the watch was left on purpose, the duo fall into a trap. After removing their utility belts, the Clock King encases our heroes in the bottom half of a giant hourglass, which is slowly filling up with sand.

The Clock King Gets Crowned. Waiting until the Clock King has left, the duo rock the hourglass back and forth until it topples over onto its side. Then, like hamsters in a cage, they begin to run inside the glass until it rolls outside and into the path of an oncoming truck, which smashes the hourglass open, releasing our heroes.

Meanwhile, Clock King discovers that one of his men accidentally planted the Automatic Energy Directional Control Switch, meant for the bomb to be used in Clock King's final caper, in the clock sold to Aunt Harriet. Realizing that his plans will be ruined unless he gets that clock back, he and his men head to Wayne Manor, where they retrieve the clock, but fail to make off with Bruce's priceless pocket watch collection, due to the sudden appearance of Bruce and Dick.

Acting on a remark made earlier by Clock King, Batman and Robin visit the giant clock atop Gotham's Clock Tower, where the timely foe plans to use the clock's mechanical blacksmith to set off a bomb, which will enable them to hijack a priceless cesium clock at exactly five o'clock. The Caped Crusaders overpower the Second Hands and capture Clock King just in the nick of time.

BatTalk

Actor Michael Pate

"Before I got to work on 'Batman,' I had seen a number of episodes that aired and thoroughly enjoyed it. When I found out that I had been cast to do something along with Walter Slezak, that to me was most intriguing.

"But it was quite a delight to work with Slezak. I knew a little about him and his family—his father particularly—but Slezak himself was a contained European personality, a very erudite, even autocratic-seeming type of person. Yet he had a very wide-ranging and sly wit that was very engaging, and he was a consummate actor.

"The whole experience proved very interesting to me, although as we rushed back and forth, and did this, that, and the next thing, and we were either chasing or being chased by Batman and Robin, I sometimes wondered what I was doing—all this while taking directions from the director."

BatFacts

- Herbert Anderson is best remembered as the father on the "Dennis the Menace" series.
- Walter Slezak committed suicide on April 22, 1983.

Special BatEquipment

Chemical Analyzer
Batphotoscope

Trivia Quiz 24

Whose birthday was celebrated in this episode?

47—An Egg Grows in Gotham
48—The Yegg Foes in Gotham

Guest Cast

Egghead—Vincent Price
Chief Screaming Chicken—Edward Everett Horton
Miss Bacon—Gail Hire
Foo Yung—Ben Weldon
Benedict—Gene Dynarski
Tim Tyler—Steve Dunne
Mayor Linseed—Byron Keith
Pete Savage—Albert Carrier
Tour Guide—Grant Woods
MacDonald—Burt Mustin
Newsman—George Fenneman
Motorcycle cop—Anthony Brand
Plainclothes cop—Ben Alexander
Lady—Mae Clarke
Policeman—Alan Emerson
Jewelry Store Clerk—Jonathan Hole
Motorist—George McCoy
Cameo (window)—Bill Dana (as Jose Jimenez)

Teleplay by Stanley Ralph Ross
Story by Ed Self
Directed by George WaGGner
Production #9717
Original air dates: 10/19/66 & 10/20/66

Plot

An Egg Grows in Gotham. In an attempt to take over Gotham City, Egghead steals the city charter from its case at City Hall. It seems the city is actually owned by the Mohican Indians and is leased to the city government. Every five years, the city must pay the Indians—in this case Chief Screaming Chicken, the last of the Mohicans—nine raccoon pelts (three pelts from each of the descendants of the city's founding fathers: Pete Savage, Tim Tyler, and our own Bruce Wayne). If the pelts are not delivered by midnight on the night the lease expires, the entire city will revert back to the Indians.

Egghead secretly signs a lease with Screaming Chicken to act as his legal representative if and when the lease should expire, which Egghead will make sure

happens. Batman and Robin trace Egghead to his hideout at the Ghoti-Oeufs Caviar Company and discover him in the middle of his negotiations with Screaming Chicken. After bombing the duo with an egg filled with laughing gas, Egghead and his gang escape.

Later that night, while Bruce, Dick, Pete Savage, and Tim Tyler are on their way to deliver the pelts to Screaming Chicken, Egghead kidnaps them. Egghead plans not only to keep the lease from being renewed by taking the group back to his hideout, but also to reveal Batman's secret identity. Using his great brain, Egghead had deduced that one of the three captured millionaires is in reality Batman. He then narrows the three down to one, Bruce. Planning to extract the truth from his brain, Egghead uses one of his ghoulish devices, which will not only transfer all of Bruce's knowledge into Egghead's brain but will leave Bruce a mindless fop as well.

The Yegg Foes in Gotham. Just as the machine has reached full power and is beginning to tap into the secrets in Bruce's mind, Dick reaches the machine's power switch and changes the machine from 110 to 220 current, causing an overload and destroying the machine. Egghead activates a radar egg bomb and then takes off. Using an overhead water pipe to make their escape, the millionaires head back to the city, where they find the deadline has come and gone. The city now belongs to Chief Screaming Chicken and Egghead.

Egghead immediately fires the city officials, banishes Batman and Robin from the city and then opens up the city to the criminal underworld. Hoping to find a way to defeat Egghead, Batman and Robin, in their guises as Bruce and Dick, steal the city charter from City Hall. They discover the charter prevents anyone with a criminal record from being a lease holder.

Egghead, having been legally deposed from office, decides to loot the city treasury

76

and escape to Venezuela. Batman and Robin arrive too late to capture Egghead, but they trace him to Old MacDonald's Chicken Farm, where Egghead is stocking up on enough Grade AAA eggs to satisfy his dietary needs before leaving the country. After an egg-throwing Batfight, Egghead and his gang are captured.

BatTalk

Actor Vincent Price

"There was a big egg fight at the end of the episode, and I was required to hit Burt Ward with an egg. The crew was fed up with Burt, so they had me throw two dozen eggs at him, and he had to stand there and take it."

Director of Photography Howard Schwartz

"Burt Ward was a nice kid, but really inexperienced, so everybody was on his case all the time, and they were kidding him, and he didn't take it very well. On the Egghead episode we got even with him. The crew got the biggest charge out of that. I was the one who egged Vincent into that. That was really funny, because Burt had eggs dripping down his face, and he was really burned, because he knew it was supposed to be one egg."

Writer Stanley Ralph Ross

"I also like writing for Vinnie Price. I liked writing for Egghead; he was a good character. The Egghead story was written by Ed Self, who is the son of William Self, and they wanted to get him into the Writer's Guild. They gave me about a three-page story, and they said, 'We will pay you the full price, but we want to get this kid into the guild.' So I wrote the script.

"I was the one who came up with all those *egg* words. Before I started the script, I looked at my thesaurus and looked up every one beginning with *ecc* or *ex*. I made a list of about seventy-five words I thought I could use. As I used them in the dialogue, I crossed them off. I think I finally used fifty or sixty of them."

BatFacts

- In order to get the pelts, Bruce had to buy a raccoon coat from a singer who had fallen on hard times.
- Egghead was considered the smartest villain in the world.
- Ben Weldon is best known for playing many villains on the old "Superman" series.

Special BatEquipment

BatFile
Sad Pill
Batcrime Computer

runny oeufs

Trivia Quiz 25

a. At what age was Bruce Wayne the marble champion of Gotham City?

b. What did Chief Screaming Chicken sell at his roadside teepee?

49—THE DEVIL'S FINGERS
50—THE DEAD RINGERS

GUEST CAST

Chandell (Fingers)— Liberace
Harry—Liberace
Doe—Marilyn Hanold
Rae—Edy Williams
Mimi—Sivi Aberg
Alfred Slye—James Millhollin
Sally—Diane Farrell
Piano Mover (Henchman)—Jack Perkins

Teleplay & story by Lorenzo Semple, Jr.
Directed by Larry Peerce
Production #9721
Original air dates: 10/26/66 & 10/27/66

PLOT

The Devil's Fingers. World-famous concert pianist Chandell, who leads a second life as the nefarious Fingers, plans to dispose of Bruce and Dick and then marry Aunt Harriet (who will be the sole surviving heir to the Wayne fortune), so he can have enough money to pay off his evil twin brother, Harry, who has been blackmailing him. Harry knows Chandell used a player piano during the White House concert, which made him famous.

As part of his plan to divert any suspicion that may fall on him, Chandell arranges for his deadly female assistants—Doe, Rae, and Mimi—to appear at Wayne Manor with their high-pitched bagpipes and put everyone to sleep (including himself) and then ransack the place.

While Bruce and Dick are away on vacation, Chandell and Harry make plans to rob the Burma Import Company with the help of his three female accomplices during his concert that evening.

During the middle of the Concert, Chandell strikes an incorrect note, signaling the girls to strike. Bruce, who had been listening to the concert on his portable radio, hears

the incorrect note, and believing something is wrong, signals Dick. The two then return to Gotham City.

Meanwhile, Chandell furthers his plan by playing up to Aunt Harriet. Later, realizing that Batman is on his trail, he leads them to a trap at twin brother Harry's Parnassus Music-Roll Co., where they are captured and tied to a conveyor belt leading directly into the machine that perforates music rolls.

The Dead Ringers. As a player piano feeds the musical notes to the music roll machine via a microphone, Batman mentally conceives of the chords that will cause the cutting devices to outline instead of puncture their bodies. The duo then outshout the piano and save their lives.

Batman and Robin quickly round up Harry and his gang of Piano Movers and transport them to police headquarters, where they reveal that a criminal named Fingers is behind it all. Harry is then sprung from jail by

his lawyer, Mr. Slye. Believing Chandell to be Fingers, Batman and Robin set a trap for him. Deducing his plan to do away with them and marry Aunt Harriet, they arrange their own deaths by faking an explosion in the darkroom set up in the front hall.

Harry and the three girls, upon learning that Chandell plans to go straight after marrying Harriet, decide to take matters into their own hands. Harry clobbers Chandell and ties him, along with Mr. Slye, whose legal fees Harry believes were too high, to the conveyor belt leading into the music roll machine.

Harry as Chandell visits Harriet, who spots him for a phony and tries to arrest him but is put to sleep (along with Alfred) by the girls' deadly bagpipes. After transporting them in a packing case, Harry machine guns the case, but is startled when Batman and Robin leap out, protected by the Batshield. They capture the gang and rescue Chandell and Slye from the music roll machine.

BatTalk

Executive Producer William Dozier

"Liberace brought his own grand piano and his own costumes. He wouldn't trust anyone else's piano."

Liberace

"Like some of the children, I loved the villains because they were sort of anti-heroes and you always wanted to see what they could do to put Batman and Robin in a predicament and then, of course, it was fun to see how they got out of it."

ABC Photograph

BatFacts

- The name *Chandell* is a play on one of Liberace's trademarks, the chandelier.
- These episodes starring Liberace were the highest-rated of all the Batman shows.

Special BatEquipment

Batgas
Wayne Manor Closed Circuit TV

Trivia Quiz 26

What was the zip code of the Parnassus Music-Roll Company?

51—Hizzonner the Penguin
52—Dizzonner the Penguin

Guest Cast

Penguin—Burgess Meredith
G.O.O.N. #1—Joey Tata
G.O.O.N. #2—Tony Epper
G.O.O.N. #3—Newell Oestreich
Mayor Linseed—Byron Keith
Gallus—George Furth
Rooper—Woodrow Parfrey
Trendek—Murray Roman
Lulu—Cindy Malone
Penguin Girl #1—Judy Parker
Penguin Girl #2—Linda Meyers
Collector—Joe Besser
Little Old Lady—Pat Tidy
Walter Klondike—Don Wilson
Chet Chumley—Dennis James
David Dooley—Allen Ludden
Little Egypt—Herself (a belly dancer)
Paul Revere & the Raiders—Themselves
Mother—Peg Shirley
Blind News Dealer—Fuzzy Knight
Cop—James O'Hara
Prisoner—John Indrisano
Moderator—Jack Bailey
Man—Benny Rubin

Teleplay & story by Stanford Sherman
Directed by Oscar Rudolph
Production #9719
Original air dates: 11/2/66 & 11/3/66

Plot

Hizzonner the Penguin. To the confusion of everyone, Penguin campaigns for the office of mayor of Gotham City. The waddling menace endears himself to the people by preventing a robbery, saving a baby in a runaway carriage, and donating a large sum of money to a city charity.

With the latest polls showing the support for Penguin to be enormous, Batman sees that the only possible way to defeat the conniving bird is to run for mayor against him.

While Batman launches a tasteful low-profile campaign, Penguin proceeds in the opposite direction, overshadowing the Caped Crusader with loud bands, pretty girls, and free champagne.

Later, when the Dymanic Duo are scheduled to appear before the Grand Order of Occidental Nighthawks, they find themselves face to face with Penguin's G.O.O.N.s. Batman and Robin are quickly overpowered, then bound, tied, and suspended on one side of a giant scale over a vat of sulphuric acid. The other side of the scale is filled with blocks of ice suspended over a giant heater. The more the ice melts, the closer our duo gets to the acid bath.

Dizzoner the Penguin. Remembering that Alfred has acid-proofed his costume, Batman leaps off the scale and into the acid, protecting his exposed face with his cape. He quickly climbs out of the vat, dissolves his bonds, and frees Robin.

Later that day, Batman's televised debate with the Penguin is interrupted by the news that the G.O.O.N.s have broken into the Gotham City Convention Hall and are making off with the priceless collection of gems set for display at the upcoming jeweler's convention. The Penguin and the Dynamic Duo rush off to thwart the crooks.

80

After a battle with the G.O.O.N.s, Penguin comes out the winner, giving him a wide lead over Batman in the subsequent election. But, as the final election returns begin to show an increase in Batman voters, Penguin realizes that his political career is coming to a close and kidnaps the board of elections members in an attempt to force the election in his favor.

Batman and Robin trace Penguin and the G.O.O.N.s to their hideout, rescue the election commissioners, and trap Penguin and his gang inside the machine used to package Penguin's campaign literature. Returning to Gordon's office, Batman resigns his new position in favor of Mayor Linseed.

BatTalk

Actor Joey Tata

"When we were doing 'Batman,' I remember we brought some people over to the set, and everybody was all excited to see the stage and the cave. Everyone was getting tickled pink looking at those people getting excited about being on the 'Batman' set. Then somebody said to me, 'Aren't you excited?' I said, 'No, this is what we do. It's our job.' Two seconds later, some old guy says to me, 'You know, the last time I worked on this lot . . .' I said, 'When?' He says, '*King Kong.*' I said, '*What?!*' He says, 'That is where the gate was that Kong came through. Right outside the stage of 'Batman' was the old forth acres where we worked.' When he said *King Kong*, I acted just like the people who were looking at the 'Batman' set, right where the Batcave was, at Desilu, which was originally RKO."

Actor Alan Napier

"I loved Penguin. My favorite moment was when Penguin was running for mayor of Gotham City, and we had this scene of wild girls and stuff. Then it cuts, and the narration says, 'Meanwhile, Batman is addressing the issues.' Then you see Batman talking to a hall, and then the camera turns around and you see three people."

BatFacts

- Paul Revere and the Raiders's presence in this episode marked the first appearance of any rock group on a sitcom.
- During the filming of this episode, Frank Sinatra paid a visit to the set, but he never did appear on the series.
- Allan Ludden and Dennis James were the hosts of the popular game shows "Password" and "P.D.Q." at the time this episode was filmed. Don Wilson is best known as Jack Benny's announcer.
- Joe Besser, seen for less than 30 seconds in the foreground (he's the one in the black suit and derby) is well known for his recurring roles on the Abbott & Costello and Joey Bishop shows, as well as for being the Curly replacement, Joe, with the Three Stooges.

Special BatEquipment

Lunar Scanning Screen
Batanalyzer
Battracer

Trivia Quiz 27

On what floor is Commissioner Gordon's office located?

53—GREEN ICE
54—DEEP FREEZE

GUEST CAST

Mr. Freeze—Otto Preminger
Miss Iceland—Dee Hartford
Mayor Linseed—Byron Keith
Shivers—Nicky Blair
Chill—Kem Dibbs
TV Newsman—Charles O'Donnell
Police Sergeant—James O'Hara
Iceman—Robert Wiensko
Little Boy—Mike Durkin
Nellie Majors—Marie Windsor
Bathing Beauty—Joan Twelve

Teleplay & story by Max Hodge
Directed by George WaGGner
Production #9725
Original air dates: 11/9/66 & 11/10/66

PLOT

Green Ice. Mr. Freeze returns to continue his plan of revenge against Batman and Robin for condemning him to live in subzero temperatures.

After escaping from prison in an ice cream truck, Mr. Freeze kidnaps Miss Iceland from the finals of the Miss Galaxy Beauty Pageant, planning to lower her body temperature to the level of his own and then take her for his bride.

Later, he makes an appearance at police headquarters and freezes Gordon, O'Hara, and their whole office. Alerted, Batman and Robin rush to Gordon's office and rescue their frigid friends. Moments later, they are confronted with a giant block of ice containing money sent by Mr. Freeze, which the local newspapers perceive as a bribe. This is the first step in Mr. Freeze's plan to discredit Batman.

Not long after, Mr. Freeze and his men make an appearance at a party being given at Wayne Manor, and after freezing everyone in the reflecting pool, two of his men arrive dressed as the Caped Crusaders and

proceed to make a mockery of the pair by losing a battle with Mr. Freeze's men. The phony heroes quickly run away in disgrace, followed by Freeze and his men. Alfred, who had been inside the house during the robbery, returns to find the frozen guests, quickly turns on the pool's heater, and releases them.

Batman and Robin trace Mr. Freeze to his hideout at a cold storage plant next to the Frosty Freezie Company factory, where they are quick-frozen by Mr. Freeze's trusty freeze gun and then transferred to the factory, where they are about to be turned into giant Frost Freezies.

Deep Freeze. Batman and Robin locate the heat exhaust valve and with their feet turn the valve so that recycled exhaust in the heating unit of the container will reverse the process of refrigeration and the resulting heat transfer will melt them free of their icy tombs.

Returning to the commissioner's office, they are greeted by a newspaper photo of Batman wearing the commissioner's gold watch, which Freeze stole during the party. Mr. Freeze's plan seems to be working as most of Gotham now believes Batman has succumbed to the temptations of bribery.

Mr. Freeze, believing that Batman and Robin are out of the way, proceeds with his master plan to blackmail Gotham City. Unless the city pays him one billion dollars, Mr. Freeze will turn Gotham City into a giant glacier. To back up his threat, Freeze demonstrates his power by freezing the Gotham City reservoir.

The Dynamic Duo secretly pay a visit to Freeze's hideout, where they are captured and about to be frozen solid. However, the duo have covered themselves with a preventive layer of Antifreeze Activating Solution. Armed with their Batthermal Underwear, they thwart Freeze's plans and overpower the frosty fiend and his men.

BATTALK

Executive Producer William Dozier

"Otto I had known for a long time, and he called me from New York and said, 'Bill, I must do a "Batman." If I don't do a "Batman," my children won't let me come home.' He hadn't acted in seventeen years, since *Watch on the Rhine* on Broadway. They [guest villians] all got the same amount of money: twenty-five hundred dollars. That's what they got, period."

Actor Alan Napier

"I had worked before 'Batman' with Awful Otto Preminger in *Forever Amber* as the English expert and dialogue director. Otto got me mad because, if anyone dried up on a close-up, he would say, 'Why don't you concentrate?' Then he comes on the set of 'Batman.' Instead of looking six foot tall, as I thought, he looks five foot tall, because it is now my territory and he is playing Mr. Freeze. It happens that I was on the set while he was doing a series of close-ups. And in every one of them Otto dried up, and it was only because of the gentleman built into my nature that I didn't say, 'Otto, why don't you concentrate?' "

Director of Photography Howard Schwartz

"We had an old-time director by the name of George WaGGner, who used to remind everybody that you spelled his name with two capital Gs, and he was directing the show that Otto Preminger did. Otto was a pretty fair director in his own right. So, he and George discussed how he was going to play a scene, and he didn't like the way George had decided to do it. So, he said, 'George, I have been in the business so many years, and I have never seen it done like this.' George turned to him and said, 'Well, Otto, now you have.' That stopped him and turned him right off."

BATFACTS

- Dee Hartford is the sister of Eden Hartford, who was married to Groucho Marx.
- We learn in this episode that Mayor Linseed's wife is named Linda, but in a third-season episode he apparently remarried, because his wife is named Millie.
- Director George WaGGner directed *The Wolfman*, which starred Lon Chaney, Jr.

SPECIAL BATEQUIPMENT

Crime Analyzers
Batthermal Underwear
Antifreeze Activating Solution

TRIVIA QUIZ 28

a. What flavors of Frosty Freezies was Mr. Freeze going to turn the Dynamic Duo into?

b. Can you name the five finalists in the Miss Galaxy Contest?

55—THE IMPRACTICAL JOKER
56—THE JOKER'S PROVOKERS

GUEST CAST

Joker—Cesar Romero
Cornelia—Kathy Kersh
Latch—Louis Quinn
Bolt—Larry Anthony
Angus Ferguson—Christopher Cary
Egbert—Alan Napier
Little Girl—Valerie Szabo
Commentator #1—Larry Burrell
Commentator #2—Clyde Howdy
Cameo (Window)—Howard Duff

Teleplay & story by Jay Thompson & Charles
  Hoffman
Directed by James B. Clark
Production #9723
Original air dates: 11/16/66 & 11/17/66

PLOT

The Impractical Joker. After committing a series of key-related crimes, the Joker steals the Jeweled Key of Kaincardine with the aid of his new invention, a mysterious little box, which leaves the Dynamic Duo completely helpless while he makes off with the key.

Later, Batman and Robin, following a clue broadcast by the Joker, track the clown to a fur salon, where they battle the funny fiend and his men. The villains manage to escape, but not before the Joker drops his little box. On closer examination, it is discovered that it contains nothing more than a bunch of wires, a battery, and a few flashing lights. The box merely acted as a diversion while the Joker hypnotized them.

Back in the Batcave, Batman uses the Batcomputer and a phone book to find the Joker's hideout. Proceeding to the hideout, they are captured by the Joker, who places Robin inside a spray wax machine, while Batman is strapped to a giant key duplicator.

The Joker's Provokers. Batman removes his duplicate house key from his utility belt and jams it into the mechanism, causing it to release him. He quickly routs the Joker's men and rescues the now immobilized Robin from the wax spray machine. Returning with Robin to the Batcave, Batman is able to return him to normal with the aid of Bat Wax-solvent.

Meanwhile, the Joker has perfected another little box. This one, along with the key-shaped pills he dropped into the city's water supply, allow the villain to control time. Demonstrating this machine for the unsuspecting people of Gotham City alerts Batman and Robin, who figure out the Joker's plan and set a trap for him at the waterworks.

Alfred, agreeing to pose for his look-alike cousin Egbert, the night watchman at the waterworks, manages to turn the little box against the Joker and his gang, freezing them in time. Batman and Robin arrive just in time to capture the Joker and his men when Alfred unknowingly turns off the device.

BatTalk

Actor Cesar Romero

"Why Dozier wanted me I'll never know because I asked his wife, Ann Rutherford, 'Why did Bill think of me for this part?' She said, 'I don't know. He said he saw you in something, and he said, "He's the one I want to play the Joker."' I haven't the slightest idea what it was they he saw me in, because I had never done anything like it before."

Executive Producer William Dozier

"We didn't have serious problems with Burt Ward. He was very young and very broke when I first saw him. We were interviewing guys, and my assistant, Charles Fitzsimons, a very able man and a very bright man who is now head of the Producer's Guild, was interviewing people. One day he came into my office and said, 'I think this may be the guy.' So, he brought this Burt Ward in. Burt introduced himself, and I said, 'He is the guy, all right, if he can walk and talk.' He and his wife were living on turned-in pop bottles. Really, literally that is what they were living on. So, we put him in the show, and he was very good. I think he was exactly right for the part. Not long after the show got started, he dumped his wife and married Kathy Kersh (the ex-wife of the guy who played Ben Casey, Vince Edwards), who was a barracuda. She ate him alive and encouraged him to spend money. He spent his money as fast as he made it, thinking it was going to last forever, and became very starstuck. He thought he was a star, but he was too young and too inexperienced to evaluate his position, whereas Adam evaluated his position completely. Adam was smart; he saved his money. He knew this was a freak thing that wasn't going to last forever. And to get the most out of it, he and Burt would go out on weekends and open supermarkets in their outfits and the Batmobile. We had three Batmobiles, and they'd clean up. They would make a lot of money on those weekend things."

BatFacts

- Kathy Kersh was Burt Ward's wife at the time this episode was filmed.
- This was the first appearance of Alfred's Alfcycle.

Special BatEquipment

Bat Wax-solvent
Counterhypnosis Batpellets
Batcapsule Dispensary

Trivia Quiz 29

a. What television show does Bruce watch in this episode?

b. What alias does the Joker use in this episode?

57—Marsha, Queen of Diamonds
58—Marsha's Scheme with Diamonds

Guest Cast

Marsha, Queen of Diamonds—Carolyn Jones
Grand Mogul—Woody Strode
Aunt Hilda—Estelle Winwood
Announcer—Hugh Douglas
Sergeant O'Leary—James O'Hara
Girl—Joyce Nizarri
Clergyman—Charles Stewart
Clerk—Ben Gage
Victim #1—Harry Stanton
Victim #2—William McLennon
Victim #3—Murray Pollack
Victim #4—Rick DiSante

Teleplay & story by Stanford Sherman
Directed by James B. Clark
Production #9727
Original air dates: 11/23/66 & 11/24/66

Plot

Marsha, Queen of Diamonds. Chief O'Hara, under the spell of the Queen of Diamonds, allows her to rob U. Magnum's of the famous Pretzel Diamond. Gordon tells the Dynamic Duo of O'Hara's odd behavior, and they race to police headquarters.

Meanwhile, Marsha has O'Hara phone Gordon, who rushes to Marsha's hideout to rescue O'Hara. Using her Aunt Hilda's love potion, administered by a dart fired from a statue of Cupid, Marsha adds Gordon to her long list of love slaves. Under Marsha's orders, Gordon phones Batman and leads him into a trap at Marsha's hideout.

Batman and Robin arrive at the hideout, where Batman is struck by a love dart. Using his superior will, Batman resists the power of the drug. Realizing she has failed, Marsha orders the Grand Mogul and her Guardians to dispatch the duo. During the fight, Marsha drugs Robin, so Batman gives up the fight. Marsha demands the Batdiamond, which powers the Batcomputer in return for the boy. Batman refuses, swearing that no

stranger will ever enter the Batcave. Marsha knows that Batman will not break his oath, so she orders him to marry her. This way, she will no longer be a stranger; she will be Mrs. Batman. The next time we see the Caped Crusader, he is walking down the aisle toward the altar, with Marsha at his side.

Marsha's Scheme of Diamonds. Just as Batman is about to say, "I do," Alfred, disguised as a British solicitor, arrives with Aunt Harriet, whom he claims is the one and only Mrs. Batman. Realizing she's been had, Marsha, along with the Grand Mogul, leaves the church in a huff. Batman and Alfred return to Marsha's hideout with the Bat-Antidote Kit to rescue Robin and the others.

Tracing Marsha to Aunt Hilda's underground lair, the duo battle Marsha's

Guardians, while Aunt Hilda tries to turn them into a variety of animals.

As both her Guardians and Aunt Hilda's potions fall by the wayside, Marsha drugs the duo, who fall to the floor unconscious. Hilda then douses the pair with her strongest potion, which is supposed to turn them into toads.

The next day, Marsha and the Grand Mogul appear in Gordon's office, carrying a cage containing two toads wearing miniature Batcapes. Marsha threatens to feed the talking toads (whose voices were actually supplied by the Grand Mogul, using ventriloquism) to her pet cat unless Gordon gives in to Marsha's demands. Just then, Batman and Robin (having escaped from Marsha's hideout) arrive to disarm the Grand Mogul and thwart Marsha's plan.

BatTalk

Actor Alan Napier

"I enjoyed the one in which I appeared as a solicitor from England with Carolyn Jones. The writers of the episode said that I was supposed to come from Putney Hill. I said there is no place called Putney Hill; there is a *Putney.* They said, "Then come from where you would like to come from.' So, I remembered one of those lovely English country names: Morton in the Marsh. An enormous thing ensued from this when it was shown in England. The inhabitants of Morton in the Marsh were up all night over the excitement of being mentioned on the 'Batman' show. It even extended to Birmingham, the city of my birth. I remember getting a call from Birmingham, England, at three o'clock in the morning, and I thought that one of my relations there had died or something. I wasn't organized after being awakened from a deep sleep and said more than I would have had I realized that this was a reporter trying to get a story. Batman appeared on the front page of the *Birmingham Post.* It is extraordinary, the power of television—particularly what successful series do. Of course, we didn't go on and on forever. It ran out of characters and situations."

BatFacts

- Aunt Hilda, who for twenty years was a chemistry professor at Vassar, was thrown out for turning the entire student body orange for a week.
- We learn in this episode that Alfred has never been married.
- It was originally announced in the *New York Daily News* that Zsa Zsa Gabor was going to play the part of Marsha.

Batman was nominated for an Emmy award in 1966 in the category of Individual Achievements in Sound Editing.

Special BatEquipment

Batdiamond
Bat-Extension Phone
Batpress
Batantidotes
General All-Purpose Antidote
Batprinter
Batradar

Trivia Quiz 30

What was the name of the law firm Alfred said he represented?

59—Come Back, Shame
60—It's the Way You Play the Game

Guest Cast

Shame—Cliff Robertson
Okie Annie—Joan Staley
Messy James—Timothy Scott
Rip Snorting—John Mitchum
Laughing Leo—Milton Frome
Hot Rod Harry—Jack Carter
Andy—Eric Shea
Little Old Lady—Kathryn Minner
Guard—James McHale
Cameo (Window)—Werner Klemperer (as Colonel Klink)

Teleplay & story by Stanley Ralph Ross
Directed by Oscar Rudolph
Production #9729
Original air dates: 11/30/66 & 12/1/66

Plot

Come Back, Shame. Shame, the conniving cowboy of crime, and his western gang plan to build a super-powered truck, which will outrace the Batmobile. Needing some additional parts for the truck, they steal a racing car right in the middle of the Gotham City 500 road race.

Shame returns to his hideout at the abandoned Westernland amusement park, where he befriends a small boy named Andy, who believes he is a real cowboy. Meanwhile, Batman has figured out Shame's scheme and plants a story with disc jockey Hot Rod Harry about the new parts added to the Wayne limousine. Shame hears the broadcast on Andy's radio and prepares to steal the limousine.

Allowing Shame to make off with the car, Batman and Robin trace the vehicle to Westernland via the Infrared Batdust, which the limousine's tires were cleverly coated with. After a battle, the duo are clobbered by a falling chandelier. Leading them outside, Shame stakes the pair out in the middle of the street and then releases a herd of stampeding cattle in their direction.

It's the Way You Play the Game. Thanks to the vibrations of the stampeding cattle, the stake holding Batman's hands shakes loose from the ground. Jumping to his feet, Batman removes his cape and, matador-style, guides the cattle away from Robin and himself.

Returning to the Batcave, Batman once again consults Hot Rod Harry, who refers them to Laughing Leo, a used car salesman and secretly a member of Shame's gang. Unable to get a straight answer from Leo, the duo depart. Feeling something is wrong, Leo reports back to Shame that the duo are still alive. Shame expects Batman to return and prepares to ambush him.

As predicted, the Caped Crusaders return to Westernland, where Robin is shot in the heel by a stray bullet. Batman rushes the boy back to the Batcave for treatment, where Alfred informs him that he is scheduled to appear at the rodeo this afternoon as Bruce Wayne. Alfred's reminder gives Batman the answer he was looking for. Shame plans to steal the four prize Black Angus bulls, each worth $300,000, that will be on display.

However, by the time the Dynamic Duo reach the rodeo, Shame has already escaped with the bulls in his super-powered truck. Figuring that the bulls will have to be fed, Batman tracks the gang to the K.O. Corral down at the stockyards, where, after a blazing gun battle, Batman and Robin corral the entire gang.

BatTalk

Actor Cliff Robertson

"I think I do kind of remember the producers making several calls ahead of time, saying, 'We would love to have you on the show.' I was doing two films, when I talked with them, and at one point they said, 'What kind of character would you like to play?' I said it might be kind of fun to play a very, very, very dumb cowboy, who took himself very, very seriously. Then they decided to do a takeoff on Shane. That is how they came up with his name, Shame. I recall they kind of let me pick my own costume, and I did a lot of my own stunts."

Writer Stanley Ralph Ross

"A lot of times the casting was not what we had imagined. I would just write the scripts and then find out Cliff Robertson was playing the part of Shame. I would have loved to have seen it played by Clint Eastwood, and he was a television actor at that time.

"There was a Shame script where I had them staked out on the ground and had these cattle about to trample them, and I couldn't figure out how to get them out of it. My son, who at the time was only about eight—and his name is Andy, which is why the kid's name was Andy—said, 'Would it make sense if all of these cattle would jar the ground enough that Batman could get his hands free?' I liked it, so that is what we used."

BatFacts

- The strangest thing about this episode is the appearance of Colonel Klink in the window. "Hogan's Heroes" was on a different network, and the fact that it was set during the 1940s made it impossible for the series to cross over. However, this didn't phase the Dynamic Duo, who go so far as to tell Klink to say hello to Colonel Hogan for them.
- John Mitchum is Robert Mitchum's younger brother.

Special BatEquipment

Precious Metals Batanalyzer
Infrared Batdust
Batroscope
Baticillin Lozenge

Trivia Quiz 31

Where was Laughing Leo's car lot located?

61—THE PENGUIN'S NEST
62—THE BIRD'S LAST JEST

GUEST CAST

Penguin—Burgess Meredith
Chickadee—Grace Gaynor
Cordy Blue—Lane Bradford
Maty Dee—Vito Scotti
Officer Hoffman—James O'Hara
Warden Crichton—David Lewis
Judge Moot—Voltare Perkins
Bailiff—Marvin Brody
Lady—Violet Carlson
Ballpoint Baxter—Stanley Ralph Ross
Cameo (Window)—Ted Cassidy (as Lurch)

Teleplay & story by Lorenzo Semple, Jr.
Directed by Murray Golden
Production #9701
Original air dates: 12/7/66 & 12/8/66

PLOT

The Penguin's Nest. Penguin opens a restaurant catering to the rich people of Gotham City. He has the wealthy customers write out their own food orders so he can legally collect handwriting samples. Upon his inevitable return to prison (the bird has been in prison so many times that he has been assigned a permanent cell) he can turn them over to Ballpoint Baxter, who resides in the cell next to Penguin's. Using the blank check forms available in the prison print shop, Baxter can forge the millionaires' signatures on the worthless checks, which Penguin will cash when he is once again released from prison.

There is only one problem with Penguin's plan: he can't seem to get arrested! First, he tried to steal a piece of jewelry from Aunt Harriet, who was dining at the restaurant, but Batman and Robin later intercede and allow the waddling menace to go free, even after he strikes Chief O'Hara in the face with a pie. Since Penguin insists on returning to prison, Batman suspects the bird is up to something sinister and decides to check his prison cell assignment. Thus he uncovers Penguin's plan and decides to allow Penguin to go free, hoping he will get careless and tip his hand.

Later, the Dynamic Duo catch Penguin in another attempt to return to prison, this time by shooting one of his own men. Batman spots the murder as a fake. The good guys arrest Penguin anyway but foil his plan by confining him in the city jail instead of the State Prison. Penguin's gang then frees him and takes Chief O'Hara as a hostage.

Penguin locks O'Hara inside a trunk suspended on a water slide over an electric swimming pool. The Dynamic Duo rush to the rescue but find themselves pinned down by machine gun fire, unable to aid the helpless O'Hara.

BatTalk
Writer Stanley Ralph Ross

"I said to Howie [producer Howie Horwitz], 'I want to be in the show.' He said, 'OK, I will give you a part, but if you think you are funny, see how funny you can be with no lines.' "

BatFacts

- The character of Ballpoint Baxter is played by writer Stanley Ralph Ross, whose nickname is Ballpoint.
- This episode is based on the original comic book story that appeared in the August/September 1946 issue of *Batman* comics.

The Bird's Last Jest. While dodging bullets under cover of the Batshield, Batman places a Batinverser over the electrical lines leading into the pool, causing the water to eject the metal trunk containing Chief O'Hara and deposit it safely on the ground. Batman then tosses some Batpellets at the gang who have run out of ammunition, knocking them out.

Penguin and his gang find themselves on trial, one step away from their goal: the state prison. Unfortunately, Penguin's scheme backfires when the judge releases them.

Batman tries to get Penguin to turn over the handwriting signatures, so he dispatches Alfred, with a false identity and a false set of fingerprints, to trick the feathered fiend. Posing as Quill-Pen Quertch, a world-famous forger, Alfred pays a visit to the Penguin's restaurant. Unluckily, Penguin recognizes Alfred and, after gassing him, dumps him inside a giant pie, which he personally delivers to Wayne Manor. Penguin threatens to bake the pie along with Alfred unless Bruce gives him $1,000,000. Pretending to fetch the money from the wall safe in the study, Bruce and Dick rush down the Batpoles and return as Batman and Robin to thwart the Penguin.

Later, in Commissioner Gordon's office, Penguin and his gang prepare to leave for the state prison (Penguin still has the handwriting samples cleverly hidden inside the handle of his trusty umbrella), when they are surprised to learn that Ballpoint Baxter has just been paroled by Bruce Wayne.

Special BatEquipment

State Pen Occupancy Report
Direct Line to Warden Crichton at Gotham City Penitentiary
Terrestrial Scanner
Batpellets
Insulated Batclippers
Batinverser
Magnifying Lens
Batpole Lift
Batpole Negate Automatic Costume Change Device

Trivia Quiz 32

What is Penguin's permanent cell number?

63—THE CAT'S MEOW
64—THE BATS KOW TOW

GUEST CAST

Catwoman—Julie Newmar
Chad Stuart—Himself
Jeremy Clyde—Himself
Eenie—Sharyn Wynters
Meanie—Tom Castronova
Miney—Chuck Henderson
Moe—Ric Roman
Benton Belgoody—Joe Flynn
Mr. Oceanbring—Jay Sebring
Harry Upps—Peter Leeds
Sir Sterling Habits—Maurice Dallimore
British Butler—Anthony Eustrez
Allen Stevens—Steve Allen
Newsman—Calvin Brown
Policeman—James O'Hara
1st Girl—Judy Strangis
2nd Girl—Cindy Ferrare
Cameo (Window)—Don Ho

Teleplay & story by Stanley Ralph Ross
Directed by James B. Clark
Production #9737
Original air dates: 12/14/66 & 12/15/66

PLOT

The Cat's Meow. Catwoman, planning to steal the voices of rock singers Chad and Jeremy, demonstrates her new Voice-Eraser by using it on a morning talk show host. She later uses her fiendish device on Commissioner Gordon, but not before he tells her where the British rock singers will be staying while in Gotham City, which turns out to be stately Wayne Manor.

In order to gain access to the mansion, Catwoman disguises herself as Miss Klutz from Duncan's Dance Studio and arranges to give Dick a free dance lesson. She quickly gasses everyone and makes her escape after she sneezes off her disguise.

Later, Batman and Robin pay a visit to the dance studio. There they do away with Catwoman's men and attempt to put the feline under arrest, but she manages to scratch both of them with a knockout drug. She then moves the unconscious duo to a giant echo chamber, where a dripping faucet, magnified ten million times, threatens to destroy their brains.

The Bats Kow Tow. The duo hum the chamber's F sharp above high C sympathtic vibration, causing the glass walls of the chamber to shatter, releasing them. Immediately, they rush to the site of Chad and Jeremy's concert, but not in time, as Catwoman has already made off with the singers' voices.

Later, Catwoman makes an appearance on the "Allen Stevens Show," where she announces that she wants $22,400,000 for the return of Chad and Jeremy's voices. The British Consul refuses to pay the ransom, leaving Batman and Robin to find Catwoman's new lair and restore their voices.

Tracing the feline felon to Mr. Oceanbring's Hair Salon, they capture the gang, but Catwoman escapes. Batman chases Catwoman to a deserted alley, where she threatens him with a sonic gun. Fortunately for our hero, Catwoman hasn't the heart to fire the gun. Batman takes the gun and puts her under arrest. She then tells him how to restore the stolen voices.

BatTalk

Actress Julie Newmar

"I remember that we did that scene in the manor late at night, and they rushed the damned scene as they always did. They never gave you a chance to do anything. You had one take, and you had to do it on that show. All I got was $1,250 a show, and there are no residuals when they play it over and over."

BatFacts

- We learn in this episode that Commissioner Gordon has grandchildren.
- One of the girls attending the concert is Judy Strangis, series production manager Sam Strangis's daughter.

Special BatEquipment

Bat Sound-Analyzer
Master Batfile
Antibat Sonic Device

Trivia Quiz 33

What television host is the character Harry Upps a parody of?

65—THE PUZZLES ARE COMING
66—THE DUO IS SLUMMING

GUEST CAST

Puzzler—Maurice Evans
Rocket O'Rourke—Barbara Stuart
Artemus Knab—Paul Smith
Blimpy—Robert Miller Driscoll
Glider—Alan Emerson
Ramjet—Jay Della
Cameo (Window)—Santa Claus

Teleplay & story by Fred De Gorter
Directed by Jeffrey Hayden
Production #9731
Original air dates: 12/21/66 & 12/22/66

PLOT

The Puzzles are Coming. The Puzzler sends Batman a challenging puzzle via a toy plane flown through Commissioner Gordon's window. Solving the puzzle, Batman concludes Puzzler is after multimillionaire Artemus Knab. Rushing to Knab's penthouse suite, they find Puzzler and Knab planning to go into the puzzle balloon business together. Returning to the Batcave with the sample puzzle balloon given to Robin by the Puzzler, the duo discover that Puzzler is planning to rob the guests at the christening party for Knab's new supersonic plane, the Retsoor. Unfortunately, they arrive too late, as Puzzler and his men have already immobilized the guests with puzzle gas and stolen their jewels. Puzzler then gasses our heroes and makes his getaway. Recovering from the gas, Batman finds the Puzzler has left another puzzle for him.

The new puzzle leads Batman and Robin, to the Puzzler's headquarters at the Globe Balloon Factory, where they are attacked by the Puzzler's men and then knocked unconscious by two toy gliders. They awaken to find themselves about to be lifted skyward by a giant hot-air balloon whose basket is scheduled to be jettisoned when the balloon reaches 20,000 feet.

The Duo is Slumming. Using a piece of gum dropped into the balloon's basket by one of Puzzler's men, Robin manages to jam the altimeter. Employing his talent for bird calls, he then attracts a hostile bird, which pecks a hole in the balloon, allowing it to glide safely to the ground. Quickly releasing themselves from their bonds, they head back to Puzzler's factory, where Puzzler buries them in balloon long enough for he and his gang to escape.

Planning to steal the Retsoor, Puzzler has his assistant, Rocket, drug Knab's tea, allowing Puzzler time to photograph Knab's detailed plans for the new plane.

Batman is alerted to the Puzzler's new target via the rooster Puzzler sent to Gordon's office (*Retsoor* is *rooster* spelled backward). He rushes to the plane's hangar, where, after a tense battle, he prevents Puzzler from stealing the plane.

BatTalk

Actor Alan Napier

"Americans call him [actor Maurice Evans] 'Maurice' but in England we call him 'Morris.' His costume was marvelous; it made him look like an old aunty. I played with Maurice about sixty years ago at the Old Vic in *Richard II*, in which he really made his name."

BatFacts

- This episode was originally entitled "A Penny for your Riddles/They're Worth a Lot More." The script was intended for the Riddler, but when Frank Gorshin no longer wanted to play the part, the writers changed it to a Puzzler story.

Special BatEquipment

Batheadphones
Secret Writing Detector

Trivia Quiz 34

What is the Puzzler's favorite trick?

67—The Sandman Cometh
68—The Catwoman Goeth
(A Stitch in Time)

Guest Cast

Sandman—Michael Rennie
Catwoman—Julie Newmar
J. Pauline Spaghetti—Spring Byington
Catarina (Policewoman Mooney)—Jeanie Moore
Snooze—Richard Peel
Nap—Tony Ballen
Female Newscaster—Gypsy Rose Lee
Tuthill—Lindsey Workman
Officer Dan Dietrich—Ray Montgomery
Officer Reggie Hogan—James Brolin
Kitty—Valerie Kairys
Catti—Pat Becker
Woman—Barbara Kelly
Policeman—William Dyer

Teleplay by Ellis St. Joseph & Charles Hoffman
Story by Ellis St. Joseph
Directed by George WaGGner
Production #9715
Original air dates: 12/28/66 & 12/29/66

Plot

The Sandman Cometh. Batman and Robin are alerted when an undercover policewoman, working as a member of Catwoman's gang, disappears shortly after warning Gordon that Catwoman is planning to commit a crime with a European criminal called the Sandman.

Later, Catwoman (in disguise), pretending to fall asleep on a mattress display in a store window, is spirited away by one of Sandman's men. She later turns up on a TV news show, where she cleverly broadcasts a commercial for the talents of a sleep expert named Dr. Somnambula (actually Sandman), in the hopes of attracting rich insomniac J. Pauline Spaghetti.

Sandman's plan works, and he is summoned to Pauline's penthouse. While examining her her, Sandman gasses her to sleep. Working quickly he photographs Pauline's financial ledger just as Batman and Robin arrive to rescue Pauline from the man they believe to be the Sandman. While Pauline proves to them that she was not in danger, Sandman makes his escape.

The duo later trace Sandman to his headquarters at the abandoned Morpheus Mattress Factory on Derwin Alley. Upon entering the building, they are surprised by Sandman and his men and are quickly captured. Batman is tied to a mattress under a giant button stitcher, while Robin (who is now under Sandman's power) is ordered to push the button that starts the machine. After starting the machine, Sandman decides to present Catwoman with Robin as a present and departs.

The Catwoman Goeth/A Stitch in Time.
As the giant needle begins its deadly work, Batman removes his utility belt, hooks it over the machine's control switch, and deactivates the machine in the nick of time. Meanwhile, Sandman has delivered Robin to Catwoman, who forces him into her tricky maze. Abandoning the Batmobile, Sandman prepares to double-cross Catwoman and elope with J. Pauline and her money.

Returning to the Batcave, Batman locates the missing Batmobile via the Batmobile Tracking Map and, with Alfred's help, recovers his car, but there is no sign of Robin. Moments later, Gordon phones and informs Batman that J. Pauline has withdrawn $200,000,000 from the bank and has eloped

with Sandman to J. Pauline Spaghetti Island.

Meanwhile, Robin has reached the middle of Catwoman's maze, where he finds the missing policewoman. Batman locates Catwoman's lair at Catacombs Condominium, Subterranean Suite Six, and informs her of Sandman's double-cross. She leads Batman to her maze, from which he returns in a matter of moments with Robin and Policewoman Mooney. As the police arrest Catwoman, Batman and Robin head for the Batboat and chart a course for Pauline's island. As Pauline shows Sandman around the now abandoned noodle factory, Batman and Robin appear. They engage Sandman and his men in a raging battle, which ends when Sandman falls into a vat of giant noodles. Our heroes soon discover that Pauline, who has been unable to sleep for seven years has fallen sound asleep standing up.

BatFacts

- The Morpheus Mattress Factory is located on Derwin Alley, which is named for assistant director Bill Derwin.
- Michael Rennie died on June 10, 1971.
- The second part of this episode has two titles due to the fact that it was re-edited to include Catwoman. Some TV prints have one title, while some have the other.

Special BatEquipment

Batmobile Tracking Map

Trivia Quiz 35

Which famous comedians do Sandman's two henchmen resemble?

BatTalk

Writer Ellis St. Joseph

"My experience with 'Batman' was a very strange one. I loved doing it, but when I came into it, it was in its second year, and its ratings were falling off. I knew why—it was very clear to me—but it wasn't to them, because I believe they were so into it. There is a delicate balance between comic or camp and suspense, and if you listen to the critics too much about the camp, you become totally comic and lose suspense. I think that kids as well as grown-ups want a little suspense along with the comedy, but they had lost it. So, I set about creating something that would restore the feeling of suspense and even increase, if possible, the comedic elements.

"When I wrote it, I tried to think of what parody to use. I have always been fascinated by the German expressionist films and, in particular, *The Cabinet of Dr. Caligari*. So, I thought of doing a Batman version of Caligari, and that is what it is. When I handed it in very quickly, I got a letter from Bill Dozier. It said: 'Dear Ellis, I want to congratulate you on writing the best "Batman" script of the series.' He said some very, very flattering things about it. Then the next paragraph was, 'As far as I'm concerned, from now on you can work at this studio for the rest of your life. Thanks and Best Wishes, Bill.'

"This was one of the nicest letters a writer ever got from a producer. So, I stayed around only long enough to say that there is only one actor, I think, who would be perfect for the villain, and that was Robert Morley, who is terrible at comedy but wonderful at wit. However, if he played it seriously, it could become witty. And to do Dr. Caligari played by Robert Morely would have been absolutely right, and it would have suspense, too. They sent the script to Morley, who agreed to play it. I knew we were going to have something explosively successful and wonderful.

"The next news was horrendous. I didn't hear from Bill, but I learned from other people that they had a commitment with the Catwoman and they didn't know how to use her. Obviously, they had to use her (I wish they had used her on another script), so they gave my script to the story editor, Charles Hoffman, and he combined the Catwoman with my version of Dr. Caligari. Now, if they had come to me, I think I could have done almost the impossible, I think I could have combined it, but I would have treated the Catwoman the way the musical treats cats; I would have made her a sinister black shadow of a cat on Halloween night. I would have used her the way I used the other characters, but they didn't do that. It was a mishmash, and of course, Morley refused to play it [Sandman] as it was no longer a star role.

"I then heard from a charming actress Spring Byington, whom I have always admired, and I got a letter that just sent me reeling. She said: 'Dear Mr. St. Joseph, I cannot tell you how I appreciate being given a role like that of J. Pauline Spaghetti.' What she was referring to was a role I wrote for John Abbott, called J. Paul Spaghetti, based on J. Paul Getty. So, this lovely woman, whom I had admired since I was a boy on the screen and stage, was telling me how grateful she was because 'so rarely a part like that comes an actress's way, and I hope to be able to tell you this personally.' I could not answer the letter. How could I tell her the things I have just told you?

"Then, of course, there was the casting of the Morley role with Michael Rennie. As far as I'm concerned, for *The Day the Earth Stood Still*, he deserves a place in history, but other than that he was a rather stiff actor, and it was not the role for him. So, what began as the best script of the series ended up a mess."

69—THE CONTAMINATED COWL
70—THE MAD HATTER RUNS A FOUL

GUEST CAST

Mad Hatter (Jervis Tetch)—David Wayne
Polly—Jean Hale
Benny—Lennie Bremen
Skimmer—Victor Ames
Professor Overbeck—Leonid Kinskey
Hattie Hatfield—Barbara Morrison
Bonbon—Jesslyn Fax
Jennings—Paul Bryar
American Operator—Heather Young
British Operator—Gil Stuart
Russian Operator—Margaret Teele
Otto Puffendorfer—Richard Collier
Maudie—Ivy Bethune
Stooge #1—Charles Picerni
Stooge #2—Roger Creed

Teleplay & story by Charles Hoffman
Directed by Oscar Rudolph
Production #9739
Original air dates: 1/4/67 & 1/5/67

PLOT

The Contaminated Cowl. Jervis Tetch, the evil Mad Hatter, has decided to stop stealing hats and instead plans to use hats to commit crimes, so he steals 700 hat boxes from BonBon's Box Boutique and puts his collection of headpieces into storage.

Alerted to the box robbery, Batman and Robin use the Batcomputer to figure out the Mad Hatter's next crime, which they correctly predict to be the robbery of Hattie Hatfield's ruby from the Headdress Ball at the Top Hat Room. The Hatter, disguised as the Three-Tailed Pasha of Panchagorum, steals the ruby just as Batman and Robin arrive, and he quickly tosses his fez to the floor, causing an explosion of fireworks. In the confusion, the Hatter manages to spray Batman's cowl with radioactive spray before he and his men escape.

Batman, protected by an Antiradioactive Batpill, rushes his contaminated cowl (which has turned bright pink from the spray) to the Atomic Energy Laboratory, where the Hatter, posing as Professor Overbeck's assistant, Otto Puffendorfer, steals the cowl, while Batman changes into a spare one. The duo are then captured and trapped by the Hatter and his men inside a giant X-Ray Accelerator Tube and Fluoroscopic Cabinet, which when activated will irradiate the duo forever.

The Mad Hatter Runs A Foul. As the Mad Hatter makes his escape, Professor Overbeck releases the duo, who survived the deadly rays with the aid of their Bat-X-Ray Deflectors, from the cabinet and replaces them with a pair of human skeletons dressed in Batcostumes. Later, when the Hatter returns to the lab and discovers the skeletons, he believes the duo are dead. And so does the rest of the world, when the lab's cleaning woman discovers the Batskeletons the next morning and alerts the police.

With Batman and Robin out of the way, the Hatter proceeds with his real crime. He plans to substitute Hattie Hatfield's ruby

Continued on next Batpage

SPECIAL BATEQUIPMENT

Batcomputer Accelerated Concentration
  Switch
Home Dry Batcleaning Plant
Antiradioactive Batpill
Bat-X-Ray Deflector
Batradar
Underwater Batsonar Device

TRIVIA QUIZ 36

How is Alfred related to the cleaning lady who discovered the Batskeletons?

99

(which he knew was a fake) for the priceless ruby from the forehead of the Golden Buddha of Bergama on display at the Gotham Art Center.

Batman and Robin trace the Hatter to his hideout at the defunct Green Derby Restaurant via the homing transmitter hidden inside the stolen cowl. Finding the Hatter and his men waiting for them atop a giant water tower adjacent to the restaurant, the duo climb up after them. After a narrow escape on the tower's ledge, the duo subdue the villains and prepare to meet the millions of people who came out to greet them upon learning they were still alive.

BatFacts

- Alfred makes all of the Batcostumes.
- This episode was based on an original comic book story that appeared in the April 1956 issue of *Batman* comics.

BatTalk

Actor Alan Napier

"I had an idea, which they wouldn't do, but I think it would have been very funny: that I am cleaning Robin's Batpole and slip, and I come down wearing Robin's costume, which is too small for me."

71—THE ZODIAC CRIMES
72—THE JOKER'S HARD TIME
73—THE PENGUIN DECLINES

GUEST CAST

Joker—Cesar Romero
Penguin—Burgess Meredith
Venus—Terry Moore
Mercury—Hal Baylor
Mars—Joe Di Reda
Saturn—Eddie Saenz
Neptune—Dick Crockett
Uranus—Charles Picerni
Leo Crustash—Charles Fredricks
Basil Bowman—Howard Wendell
Salesman—Louis Cordova
Truck Driver—Vincent Barbi
1st Zoologist—Jonathan Kidd
2nd Zoologist—Milton Stark
Delivery Boy—Rob Reiner

Teleplay by Stanford Sherman
Story by Stephen Kandel
Directed by Oscar Rudolph
Production #9733
Original air dates: 1/11/67, 1/12/67 & 1/18/67

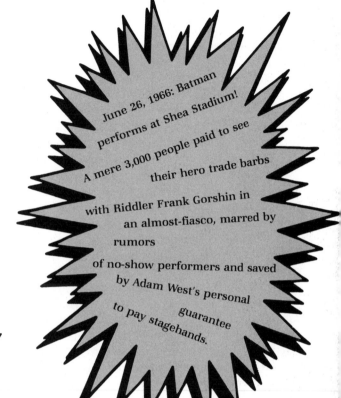

June 26, 1966: Batman performs at Shea Stadium! A mere 3,000 people paid to see their hero trade barbs with Riddler Frank Gorshin in an almost-fiasco, marred by rumors of no-show performers and saved by Adam West's personal guarantee to pay stagehands.

PLOT

The Zodiac Crimes. The Joker pays a visit to Commissioner Gordon's office and steals a Rare Art Map. Alerted, Batman and Robin deduce that the Clown Prince of Crime is planning to commit twelve crimes based on the signs of the zodiac and that he already committed the first one when he stole the Rare Art Map, whose initials stand for the sign of the Ram.

Meanwhile, back at his hideout, the Joker clues the recently arrived Penguin into his nefarious astrological plan. Batman and Robin, believing the Joker is planning to kidnap a singing duo named the Twins (Gemini), rush to their side. Unknown to our duo, the singers have been replaced by the

Continued on next Batpage

SPECIAL BATEQUIPMENT

Batknife
Parachute Jettison Button
Batmobile Parachute Pickup Service
Batanalyst
Batradar
Police Radio Cut-in Switch
Batspectrograph Criminal Analyst
Emergency Battrunk Lock
Special Exploding Batarang
Portable Batlab
Mobile Phone Batplugs
Batprobe Negative Ion Attractor

TRIVIA QUIZ 37

What flavor is the Joker-Jelly?

Joker's aides, and Penguin is waiting to trap them. Arriving at the studio, the duo are led outside, where Penguin escapes on the Joker's Boom Bug. Racing to the Batmobile, Batman and Robin chase the bizzare truck, while the Penguin cleverly lifts himself off the truck with the aid of his trusty umbrella and an overhead wire. While the Dynamic Duo are led on a wild goose chase, the Joker and his aide, Venus, make off with the real twins, the famous Twin Diamonds.

Returning to the Batcave, Batman learns the location of the Joker's hideout by analyzing the wig Venus left behind at the studio when she pretended to be one of the Twins. Arriving at the hideout, Batman finds the place deserted except for Venus, who, having fallen for Batman, agrees to help them capture Joker. She leads the duo to the opera house, where Joker plans to commit two zodiac crimes by kidnapping Leo Crustash (the Lion and the Crab). A fight ensues and Penguin is captured, but Joker escapes.

Figuring that Joker will plan to steal a masterpiece entitled *Virgin Bereaved* (Virgo), they rush to the Gotham City Museum, where they are captured and tied to an altar beneath a giant meteorite, which is rigged to fall on them when its supporting cable is cut by a revolving piece of thermite attached to a planetary mobile surrounding the great rock.

The Joker's Hard Time.
Having freed one of his hands, Batman takes the Batarang from his utility belt and throws it at the burning thermite. Breaking off a piece, Batman uses it to burn them free of their bonds seconds before the great stone drops.

Joker believes the duo are finished and makes off with the statue of Justice (Libra) from outside police headquarters, while Venus makes off with a jeweled scorpion (Scorpio). Batman and Robin arrive at police headquarters in time to give chase to the Joker, who has made his escape in a stolen police car.

Unable to catch him, they set a trap for him at the home of Basil Bowman (Sagittarrius the Archer). When the Joker arrives and finds the Dynamic Duo, he grabs Venus and, with a knife at her throat, makes his escape using Venus as a shield.

Realizing Joker is not to be trusted, Venus switches to Batman's side and leads him to a record shop, where they find Leo Crustash. Later, not only does Joker make off with two rare fish (Pisces) that were on exhibit at the park fountain, but one of his men manages to capture Venus as well. Back at his headquarters, Joker sets a trap for the Caped Crusaders who are caught in a huge net upon entering the hideout and are quickly transferred to a water-filled tank, where, along with Venus, they are about to be eaten by a giant clam. The Joker leaves to prepare his next crime, while Robin is swallowed by the clam.

The Penguin Declines.
Batman breaks free of his chains, rushes over to the clam, and pries it open long enough to rescue Robin. Freeing Venus, they make their escape, while the Joker, who needs his help with his remaining crimes, smuggles the Penguin out of jail in a laundry truck.

Using a mixture of his own creation, Joker turns the entire Gotham City water supply (Aquarius) into Joker-Jelly, refusing to change it back unless he is paid $10,000,000. Meanwhile, Penguin, claiming to have reformed, tries to romance Venus (who is staying at Bruce Wayne's midtown apartment) into asking Batman to let her visit the Batcave, so she can remove Penguin's criminal record from the Batcomputer for him.

After turning the Joker-Jelly back into water with the aid of a Special Exploding Batarang and the Portable Batlab. Batman and Robin pay a visit to Venus. Believing Penguin's story about going straight, she convinces Batman into taking her to the Batcave.

Hoping to make Batman the goat (Capricorn), Penguin, Joker, and his men secretly hide inside the Batmobile's trunk. When Batman returns with Venus to the Batcave, they pop out, ready to do battle. After a fierce fight, the gang is captured and ready to be handed over to the police.

BatFacts

- After stealing the art map, the Joker gives a false clue to Batman to the effect that "Taurus the Bull is next on my show," and "You'll be singing a song of woe." Joker was telling Batman a lot of bull, because his real objective was Gemini, the Twins, a new singing duo who sing a song of woe.

- Terry Moore is best remembered for her role in the film *Mighty Joe Young*.
- With the exception of the last three, all of the crimes were committed in the correct order of the signs of the zodiac. The last three crimes were done in reverse zodiac order.
- "All in the Family" costar Rob Reiner made one of his first TV appearances in Part 3 of this story.

74—That Darn Catwoman
75—Scat, Darn Catwoman

Guest Cast

Catwoman—Julie Newmar
Pussycat—Leslie Gore
Spade—Jock Gaynor
Marlowe—Tony Epper
Templar—George Sawaya
Pat Pending—J. Pat O'Malley
Rudy (Valet)—Steve Franken
Prince Ibn Kereb—David Renard
Girl Teller—Rolla Altman
Little Al—Allen Jenkins

Teleplay & story by Stanley Ralph Ross
Directed by Oscar Rudolph
Production #9743
Original air dates: 1/19/67 & 1/25/67

Plot

That Darn Catwoman. After giving a speech at Aaron Burr High School, Robin is drugged by Catwoman's young aide, Pussycat. The drug, called Cataphrenic, turns Robin to evil. After roughing up Chief O'Hara, the Boy Wonder departs as the new member of the Catwoman gang.

O'Hara quickly reports back to Gordon, who alerts Batman. Meanwhile, upstairs in the manor, Catwoman, Robin, and her men make off with the $200,000 Bruce keeps on hand as house money.

Aware that the police are on her trail, Catwoman calls Batman (through Gordon's office) and threatens to kill Robin if the police interfere. After robbing a local bank and the home of inventor Pat Pending, Batman deduces that Catwoman will next try to rob a weighing-in ceremony for a visiting Arabian prince.

Batman arrives to do battle with the Catmen, but when he finds he must now fight Robin, he allows the boy to win the fight. Later, Batman traces Catwoman to her hideout, where he is tied to a giant mousetrap that will spring shut just as soon as Robin finishes cutting the rope.

Scat, Darn Catwoman. Catwoman agrees to release Batman from the trap if he will agree to join her gang. Having little choice, Batman agrees, but he takes a Batantidote pill prior to being drugged with Cataphrenic, which allows him to keep his free will. Pretending to be under Catwoman's spell, Batman follows Catwoman to an old criminal's home, where she purchases a set of plans to the Gotham City Mint.

Batman secretly phones the police and informs them where they can capture Robin and Pussycat. Knowing that Robin is now safe, Batman plans to set a trap for Catwoman, who convinces him to take her back to the Batcave.

While in the Batcave, Batman leaves a note for Alfred ordering him to deliver the Batantidote to Robin at police headquarters.

Returning to the city, they meet the rest of the gang at the mint. Using a hidden entrance detailed in Catwoman's plans, they enter the building and plan to loot the safe. After blasting the safe open with a silent explosive, they find Robin hidden inside. The duo then battle it out with the Catmen. Unaware that Catwoman has stolen his keys, Batman is surprised when Catwoman escapes in the Batmobile. Following her in O'Hara's squad car, the duo use the Batmobile's Remote Control to stop the car in front of a waterfront building. Climbing to the roof to avoid capture, the Catwoman accidentally slips, falls, and disappears into the water below—but not before proposing marriage to Batman (which he rejects only when Catwoman suggests killing Robin to make their lives together "purrfect").

BATTALK

Writer Stanley Ralph Ross

"I had used some obscure dirty words in the scripts—obscure in other languages. And they got some flack. They got some letters from people who thought it was funny that I used these obscure dirty words. But the network warned me not to do that again, and I said I wouldn't. Then I was doing a show where they had this sheik that had to be weighed. I called him the Missentiff of Furderber. Furderber is a friend of mine, Skip Furderber, and Missentiff I got from W. C. Fields. Well, the network said that sounds dirty, so I changed it to Sheik Ibn Kereb which in Arabic means 'son of a bitch.' They never caught it."

BATFACTS

- Leslie Gore is producer Howie Horwitz's niece.

SPECIAL BATEQUIPMENT

Batantidote Pill
Bathandkerchief
Automatic Batalarm for Detecting Phone-Detecting Equipment
Diversionary Batphone Lines

TRIVIA QUIZ 38

Which president does Batman speak to on the phone?

76—Penguin is a Girl's Best Friend
77—Penguin Sets a Trend
78—Penguin's Disastrous End

Guest Cast

Penguin—Burgess Meredith
Marsha, Queen of Diamonds—Carolyn Jones
Aunt Hilda—Estelle Winwood
Major Beasley—Bob Hastings
General MacGruder—Alan Reed, Jr.
Miss Patterson—Kimbery Allen
Henchmen #1—Frank Baron
Mr. Tambor—Milton Stark
Truck Driver—Ted Fish
Henchman #2—Frank Conte
1st Guard—Don Hannum
2nd Guard—Andy Romano
Workman—Brad Logan

Teleplay & story by Stanford Sherman
Directed by James B. Clark
Production #9741
Original air dates: 1/26/67, 2/1/67 & 2/2/67

Plot

Penguin is a Girl's Best Friend. Batman and Robin accidentally interrupt a holdup scene Penguin is shooting for his new movie and find themselves forced to sign a contract to appear in the film.

Batman arranges for Aunt Harriet's Film Decency League to raid the scene in which Marsha is supposed to take a nude milk bath. So, Penguin tries to teach Batman a lesson by arranging a love scene between Batman and the Queen of Diamonds so that he can deliberately film one hundred takes of the pair kissing.

While Marsha and her Aunt Hilda go off in search of old toads for one of Hilda's love potions, Penguin moves his movie company to the Museum of Antiquities, where his men make off with the entire collection of priceless 15th-century chainmail armor.

When Penguin finds out that Batman knows he stole the armor, he arranges a staged fight in which the duo are beaten up for real. He then moves the heroic pair outside to a giant catapult, where he straps a camera to their legs and prepares to launch them on a trip across town.

Penguin Sets a Trend. As the rope holding the catapult slowly burns through, Batman remembers that he still has the Batmobile's remote control device strapped to his arm. Quickly, he figures out the exact point where Robin and he will come crashing down. Then, using the remote control, he signals the car to meet them there. As the duo are launched into the air by the catapult, the Batmobile heads for its programmed destination. The car finally reaches the correct spot in time to release a safety net from the trunk, just as the Dynamic Duo come down to earth.

The duo return to Penguin's movie studio, where the Penguin dresses them in two suits of armor and then immobilizes them with a huge electromagnet, leaving them to struggle while he keeps an appointment with General Magruder at the Hexagon.

Batman somehow manages to loosen the fitting from the suit of armor and, throwing it into an open light socket, overloads the circuit and shorts out the fuse, deactivating the magnet. With no time to lose, they drive off to the Hexagon, still wearing the armor.

Meanwhile, Penguin and his men use the stolen armor to break into the secret storeroom and make off with some top-secret plans.

Arriving at the Hexagon too late to capture the Penguin, the duo pick up his trail and locate Penguin's truck. Due to the extra weight of the armor, the truck blows a tire. Abandoning the truck, Penguin sends his men with the plans back to the hideout, while he leads the duo into a trap. Leading them down an alley, he trips the armored heroes by rolling several metal drums into their path. Penguin then arranges for a passing scrap truck to cart the armored duo away to be crushed inside a high-pressure hydraulic scrap-metal crusher.

Penguin's Disastrous End. While inside the crusher, Batman reaches his utility belt and pulls out the Batpumps to counter the external pressure of the crusher. They then use a torch to cut their way free of the surrounding scrap metal. Meanwhile, Marsha and Aunt Hilda, having found their old toads, create a batch of love potion to use on the guards at the Sub-Treasury, and while the Queen of Diamonds distracts the guards, Penguin and his men move some mysterious equipment inside the gold vault.

In the meantime, Batman has tracked Aunt Hilda's escaped lizards back to her underground hideout, where they find the missing armor and one of Penguin's men, who tips them off to the Penguin's present location. They secure the Fink and head for the Sub-Treasury, just as Penguin and his gang lock themselves inside the vault for three days, after which they burst out of the building in a solid gold tank, built from the stolen Hexagon plans and gold in the vault. Batman and Robin follow with the Batzooka and disable the tank. The villains quickly surrender.

BatTalk

Director of Photography
Howard Schwartz

"There was a feud between Burt and Adam about coming on to the set. Neither one of them wanted to be there ahead of the other. So, the assistant directors always had a bad time about getting both of them on the set. You would have to bring them on at the same time."

BatFacts

- Alan Reed, Jr., is best remembered as the voice of Fred Flintstone.

According to the Soviet satire magazine "Krokodil," Batman and Robin look "like idealized representatives of the F.B.I." It accused the "caped crusader" of "deepening the spiritual vacuum of the United States." (Sept. 11, 1966)

Special BatEquipment

Batradarscopes
Homing Devices
Batzooka
Batmobile's Remote-Control Activator
Batpumps
Bat Sound-Amplifier

Trivia Quiz 39

What is the name of the monster in Aunt Hilda's cauldron?

79—BATMAN'S ANNIVERSARY
80—A RIDDLING CONTROVERSY

GUEST CAST

Riddler—John Astin
Anna Gram—Deanna Lund
Across—Jim Lefebvre
Down—Ken Scott
Professor Avery Evans Charm—Martin Kosleck
Mayor Linseed—Byron Keith
Newsie—Eddie Quillan
Reporter—Bud Furillo
TV Announcer—Tom Kelly

Teleplay & story by William P. D'Angelo
Directed by James B. Clark
Production #9745
Original air dates: 2/8/67 & 2/9/67

PLOT

Batman's Anniversary. On an urgent call from the Commissioner, Batman and Robin rush to the Gotham Plaza Hotel, where they are surprised by a party being held in honor of Batman's anniversary of cooperation with the law. During the presentation of a solid gold calf filled with $200,000, intended for charity, the party is interrupted by erupting clouds of green smoke. Then, out of nowhere, three emergency firemen appear and make off with the calf through an open window. Before making his escape, one of the firemen reveals himself to be Riddler in disguise.

The duo try to follow in the Batmobile but lose the truck in some Riddler-planned confusion. Following up on a clue left by the Riddler, the duo examine a crossword puzzle in the local newspaper. Believing they have solved the puzzle, they call Gordon to alert him. However, Gordon informs them that the underground vault of the Gotham City Bank has been flooded. Realizing they misread the clues, the duo track the Riddler to the bank, where he and his men (in wetsuits) are trying to make off with the money. Armed with their Batrespirators, the duo battle the gang underwater. During the fight, the Riddler manages to rip off Robin's Batrespirator, causing Batman to rush to his aid, giving the Riddler and his men a chance to escape.

Returning to his hideout at the soon-to-be-opened Noman Jigsaw Puzzle Factory, we learn that Riddler is trying to collect $3,000,000 so he can purchase a deadly weapon called a De-Molecularizer from inventor Professor Charm.

Meanwhile, the duo find that they have an appointment with the Gotham City's Baker's Guild to pose for lifesize marshmallow figures, which will top a giant cake. Unknown to the duo, the Riddler and his men have taken the place of the guild members. After being lifted mechanically to the top of the three-story cake, Batman and Robin find themselves trapped by the Riddler as the cake is made of quicksand. As Batman and Robin slowly sink to their deaths, the Riddler leaves to prepare his next crime.

A Riddling Controversy.
As the quicksand has almost consumed our heroes, they activate their experimental Heel and Toe Batrockets, which rocket them to safety.

Acting on another clue, Batman traces the Riddler to the home of a wealthy exiled South American dictator named Anthony Aquila, where they find Riddler robbing the safe. As the duo prepare to arrest him, Riddler leads them to a deadly explosive puzzle cage containing the dictator. Fearing for the life of the trapped man, they allow the Riddler to escape with the money. Robin solves the puzzle of the cage and releases the man, only to find that the box containing the explosives was a fake.

Having finally collected enough money, Riddler buys the professor's invention, which he prepares to demonstrate on a park statue. Disguised as a street cleaner, Riddler makes the statue disappear right under the noses of Batman and the police.

The Riddler then threatens to destroy police headquarters unless the criminal statutes are rescinded. Upon solving Riddler's last clue, Batman and Robin use the Batcopter to seed the clouds above Gotham City with di-chloride, neutralizing the Riddler's device with a well-time lightning bolt from a passing storm cloud.

Tracing the Riddler to his hideout, they quickly capture the gang. Later, in Gordon's office, a guilt-ridden Professor Charm returns the stolen money.

BatFacts

- This episode was based on a story featured in the October 1948 issue of the *Batman* comic book.
- John Astin is better known as Gomez on "The Addams Family" TV series.

BatTalk
Director of Photography
Howard Schwartz

"The series was a great opportunity for me, colorwise. I hadn't done too much color, and that was about the time when color was getting real popular. So, this was a crazy show, and you could do anything with colors. The more you did, the better they like it. So, we used every colored gel in the book."

Special BatEquipment

Batrespirators
Bat MO & ID Computer
Heel and Toe Batrockets
Remote Batcomputer Switch

Trivia Quiz 40

What article of clothing does Professor Charm demonstrate his new invention on?

81—The Joker's Last Laugh
82—The Joker's Epitaph

Guest Cast

Joker—Cesar Romero
Josie Miller—Phyllis Douglas
Mr. Glee—Lawrence Montaigne
Boff—Clint Ritchi
Yock—Ed Deemer
Mr. Flamm—J. Edward McKinley
Miranda Fleece—Hollie Haze
Dr. Floyd—Oscar Beregi

Teleplay by Lorenzo Semple, Jr.
Story by Peter Rabe
Directed by Oscar Rudolph
Production #9747
Original air dates: 2/15/67 & 2/16/67

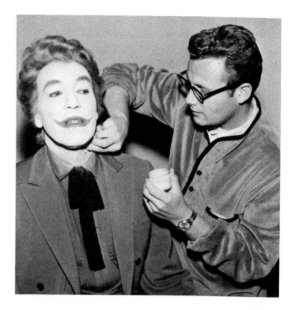

Plot

The Joker's Last Laugh. When counterfeit money is discovered coming from the Gotham National Bank, Batman and Robin are called into action. At police headquarters, they discover that the Joker has planted a tiny loudspeaker on the commissioner which has been driving Gordon crazy with a constant broadcast of laughter. Believing the Joker is behind the counterfeit money at the bank, the duo rush to the scene.

Arriving at the bank, they discover that one of the bank's teller's has been replaced by Mr. Glee, one of Joker's lifelike robots. Batman disables the robot and takes him back to the Batcave. The Joker uses the robot's retrieving signal to trace Batman's route to the Batcave, but Batman realizes he is being followed and activates the tracking signal Batdeflector to send the fiend on a false trail.

Back in the Batcave, Batman locates Joker's new hideout, at the offices of Penthouse Comic Book Publishers. In order to prove that the Joker is the counterfeiter, Bruce pretends he has embezzled some of the bank's money. If the Joker would agree to print some of his funny money, Bruce would in return make him a vice president of the Gotham National Bank. Joker quickly agrees, but just as he is about to print the money, Robin appears but is quickly subdued by the Joker's robots. He is then tied underneath the giant printing press Joker uses to make his comic books. And just to make sure that Bruce does not try a double-cross, he orders his robots to force him to throw the lever that activates the press.

The Joker's Epitaph. Just as it looks like the end for the Boy Wonder, trusty Alfred, dressed in a spare Batsuit, Batclimbs to the Joker's hideout, enters the window, and hits the villains with a douse of Batgas. As the Joker and his aide, Josie, flee with the robots, the light-fingered clown makes off with the document naming him an officer of Gotham National Bank.

The next time the duo pay a visit to the bank, they discover that Joker, under the alias W. C. Whiteface, has installed his deadly robots as the new bank tellers. Un-

110

able to take legal action, the duo return to Wayne Manor. There they meet with Joker and Josie, who now plan to blackmail Bruce with a secret tape recording of Bruce's demand for counterfeit cash. In return for the tape, he must turn over the lifeless bodies of Batman and Robin. Refusing, Joker then orders Bruce to marry Josie, with the initial marriage settlement to be $3,000,000. Unable to refuse without giving away his secret identity, Bruce, with the help of Dick, tries to find another way out.

Back in the Batcave, Batman and Robin devise a plan to use the Joker's own robots against him. While Robin readies the robots, Bruce is summoned upstairs, where he is arrested. Believing Bruce was out of his mind when he appointed the Joker to the bank, Gordon calls in a specialist named Dr. Floyd, who orders Bruce put away.

Alfred quickly heads to the Batcave to inform Robin. After giving the robots their final instructions, Robin and Alfred drive off in the Batmobile to rescue Bruce. Locating the van, they blast open the doors with the Batray and then use the super-powered Batmagnet to attract the metal buckles of Bruce's straitjacket to pull him from the speeding van. Bruce escapes harm by rolling with the fall. Dressing in his spare Batsuit, the duo rush to the bank, arriving just in time to watch the robots go into action. After Mr. Glee identifies Josie as his long-lost wife, Batman accuses Joker of aiding and abetting attempted bigamy. Then, acting on Batman's preprogrammed instructions, Boff and Yock (the robot tellers) start holding up the customers.

Realizing something has gone wrong, the Joker pulls out his robot control device and reprograms the robots to get the Dynamic Duo. Batman and Robin seize their first opportunity in this encounter to pin a crime on the Joker, quickly dispatching the mechanical menaces and arresting the felonious funnyman for attempted murder.

Later, Dr. Floyd pronounces that the fall from the van restored Bruce's sanity and gives him a clean bill of health.

BATTALK

Actor Alan Napier

"I understand why they cast Burt Ward. He was already twenty-one but sounded like fifteen. I do remember one time we were doing some soundtrack dubbing, and he had to do it over several times, and he was complaining that he was losing his voice. So, I said, 'Look, Burt, after all this nonsense is over, if you like, I will teach you to talk and perhaps even to act.' He said, 'Gee, am I that awful?' But he was a nice boy, really."

Actor Cesar Romero

"It [the Joker] was the kind of a part where you could let go, let loose, and not be yourself and all—just howl and have a lot of fun. That is what I did with the character."

BATFACTS

- Lawrence Montaigne is known to "Star Trek" fans as Stonn, Spock's rival for the hand of T'Pring in the episode "Amok Time."

SPECIAL BATEQUIPMENT

Integro-Differential Robot Analyzer
Batspot Analyzer
Criminal Business Index
Batgas
Batfan
Super-Powered Batmagnet
Batray
Tracking Signal Batdeflector
Bat Detector—Super Laughtrack Sensitivity Switch

TRIVIA QUIZ 41

Who arrests Bruce Wayne when it has been decided that he is insane?

83—CATWOMAN GOES TO COLLEGE
84—BATMAN DISPLAYS HIS KNOWLEDGE

GUEST CAST

Catwoman—Julie Newmar
Freddy (Touche) the Fence—Jacques Bergerac
Cornell—Paul Mantee
Penn—Sheldon Allman
Brown—Paul Picerni
Amber Forever—Whitney Blake
Warden Crichton—David Lewis
Alma Mater—Jan Burrell
Cameo (Window)—Art Linkletter

Teleplay & story by Stanley Ralph Ross
Directed by Robert Sparr
Production #9749
Original air dates: 2/22/67 & 2/23/67

PLOT

Catwoman Goes to College. Upon her release from prison, Catwoman enrolls as a criminology major at Gotham City University. Aided by three overage freshmen named Brown, Cornell, and Penn, she arranges for the lifesized statue of Batman to be stolen from the university rotunda. Alerted by Gordon to the theft of the statue, the Dynamic Duo arrive on the scene. While Batman examines the only clue to the theft, a freshman beanie containing a single red hair, Catwoman uses the stolen statue as the model for a Batman costume for Cornell, who so costumed is an exact double for the Caped Crusader.

The next day, Batman gives a lecture in criminology to Catwoman's class, where he gives a complete description of the statue thief. Believing Batman is on to him, Penn (who lost the beanie) makes his escape as Catwoman secretly rings the class bell.

Later, when Batman and Catwoman are sharing a soda at a local school hangout, Robin informs Batman about the recent robbery of a supermarket by a crook wearing a Batman suit. Before he can investigate, Captain Courageous, a police officer from California (who never heard of Batman) has him arrested. While Batman waits in jail, Catwoman incites a student riot. Alfred, disguised as Batman's lawyer, arrives at the jail with the Batmakeup Case, and, after a quick switch, Batman leaves the jail disguised as Alfred. That night at a rally in Chime Square, Catwoman captures the duo. After depositing them inside a giant coffee cup, she activates the mechanical percolator that, in a matter of moments, will cover our heroes with deadly sulphuric acid.

Batman Displays His Knowledge. As the acid begins to spill out of the pot's spout, Batman positions his hands under the flow so that the first few drops of acid will burn away his bonds. Then, using the Batrope, he turns off the master switch.

Meanwhile, Catwoman and her men have managed to steal the rare Batagonian Cat's Eye Opals from the Forever Jewel Company. They take them to French Freddy Touche, a well-known fence who runs a fencing school, in the hopes of selling them on the black market. Freddy knows that the opals are supposed to be jinxed and refuses to take them.

Later, while trying to convince Catwoman to return the opals for the reward, Freddy discovers that the gems are fakes, created by Batman. Infuriated, Catwoman invites Batman to meet her alone at the model home of the Sherlock Homes Real Estate development at midnight.

Arriving at the house, Catwoman tries to kill Batman with poisonous perfume, but is foiled. (Batman suspected trouble and protected himself by putting Batplugs in his nostrils.) Failing to kill Batman, Catwoman calls for her cleverly hidden henchmen to finish him off. Robin quickly appears, and together the duo rout the felons.

BATFACT

- Jacques Bergerac is now the president of Revlon in Paris.

BATTALK
Actress Julie Newmar

"I remember doing an entire sequence that even to this day amazes me, because it was six, seven, or eight minutes long. The dialogue in it was a seduction of Batman, and I remember it was late in the day, and there was no rehearsal. You would just go out there and shoot it, which is probably why I was good, because being a dancer and choreographer, when it comes to movement, I know how to cover space and use good timing and hit every mark that the camera needs me to hit. So, I would never miss a point, and I would also do everything in one take. You see, they did everybody in one take, and the people that didn't come off right the first time were winging it. The fact that it came off at all was a miracle.

"There were elements in it that were miraculous. The casting of Batman and Robin was miraculous, and certain other characters were perfectly wonderful. People met for the first time, they put it on film, and, wham-bang, it was done. It was remarkable.

"You got a sense of the rhythm, the sense of the straightness of it. You played it very, very straight. Those people who camped it up too much spoiled it. Many people, even good actors, had a tendency to ham it somewhat, and it didn't need to be, because it was already campy. The only thing you did add into it was the deliciousness of what you were up to. So, if you were strangling Batman, or if you were putting the pins into him or whatever it was you were trying to do to kill him, you enjoyed it."

SPECIAL BATEQUIPMENT

Batmake-up
Batcalendar
Well-Known Criminal's File
Batsyllable Device
Batplugs

TRIVIA QUIZ 42

In what film did guest star Paul Mantee team up with Adam West?

GUEST CAST

Colonel Gumm—Roger C. Carmel
Britt Reid/Green Hornet—Van Williams
Kato—Bruce Lee
Pinky Pinkston—Diane McBain
Cancelled—Seymour Cassel
Reprint—Rico Cattani
Block—Alex Rocco
Mr. Stample—Harry Frazier
Police Sergeant Semple—James O'Hara
1st Model (Angelique)—Angelique Pettyjohn
2nd Model (Shirley)—Jan Watson
Waiter—Dusty Cadis
Cameo (Window)—Edward G. Robinson

Teleplay & story by Charles Hoffman
Directed by Oscar Rudolph
Production #9751
Original air dates: 3/1/67 & 3/2/67

PLOT

A Piece of the Action. The Green Hornet and Kato trace a flood of counterfeit stamps to the Pink Chip Stamp Company in Gotham City. The duo confront evil foreman, Colonel Gumm, who informs boss Pinky Pinkston, who in turn asks Gordon for help.

Later, Pinky (as evil Gumm eavesdrops) asks Bruce to get Batman to guard her factory against the Green Hornet.

Bruce and Britt Reid (Hornet's alter ego) visit Boris Severoff's Stamp Store to complain about counterfeit stamps. Severoff (Gumm in disguise) denies everything, but warns his men at the factory immediately. Unfortunately, Pinky overhears the conversation and is tied up in Gumm's office.

That night, both the Dynamic Duos are overpowered and captured by Gumm and his men. The Green Hornet and Kato are fed to Gumm's giant Enlarged Perforation and Coiling Machine to become lifesized stamps, while Batman and Robin await their turn, stuck to Gumm's undetachable glue pad.

Batman's Satisfaction Green Hornet and Kato are stamped, but Batman and Robin come unglued and overpower Gumm. Batman quickly deactivates the machine and loosens the outside panel, giving the Green Hornet (stuck inside) enough room to use his Hornet gun to blast the machine open.

Green Hornet and Kato try to pick up the trail of the escaped Gumm; meanwhile, Batman discovers and (with the Batcomputer) deciphers the message Pinky left for him in Colonel Gumm's bowl of alphabet soup. The duo trace Gumm to the International Stamp Exhibition; meanwhile, Pinky has freed herself from Gumm's warehouse with the aid of her pink dog, Apricot, alerts Gordon, and accompanies the police to the exhibition.

At the exhibition, Batman and Robin find not only Gumm and his men but also the Green Hornet and Kato, whom the duo believe are villains. As the two heroic teams fight each other, Colonel Gumm, still disguised as "Mr. Barbosa," kidnaps Pinky and tries to make off with the priceless stamps. The Dynamic Duo break off their fight to rescue Pinky, and the Green Hornet an Kato make their escape.

BatFacts

- *The following is excerpted from the October 1979* Fighting Stars *magazine article "How Bruce Lee Fought his way to Hollywood" written by M. Uyehara.*

"As long as both shows were so popular among the viewers, a Kato-Robin confrontation was unavoidable. The young public was clamoring for one.

'The director decided we should participate in the Batman series instead of ours,' Bruce Lee said. He had no idea what the director had in mind, but after reading the script, he grinned and whispered to himself, 'This is great. Kato finally gets to fight Robin.'

"Bruce was a great kidder. He relished playing jokes. Especially on someone he did not care for. On the day Kato was to fight Robin, Bruce put on his most solemn face. He walked around as though carrying a heavy burden on his shoulders. He hardly said anything and did not kid around with the crew in his usual manner. He was not the same Bruce Lee everyone knew.

"On the Batman set Bruce continued his pretense. He stood in a fighting stance, teeth clenched and eyes squinted behind Kato's mask. Meanwhile, Ward as Robin, stood a good distance away from him and attempted to calm him with irrelevant comments which Bruce just ignored. Finally, the director orderd them to proceed and the camera began to roll. Bruce held his deadpan expression and inched his way toward his opponent. Ward kept his distance and yelled, 'Bruce, remember this is not for real. It's just a show!'

"Bruce later related the incident. 'I had a hard time keeping a straight face,' he said. 'I started to crowd Burt and he began to flap his elbows and jump around me. I was really keeping him scared and I hear someone in the back whisper, 'The black panther and the yellow chicken.' At that point, I burst out laughing. I just couldn't keep a straight face anymore.'

"The director didn't want to upset any fans so he cleverly let the heroes fight to a draw. Bruce viewed the whole event with amusement. 'Lucky for Robin that it was not for real; otherwise he would have been one dead bird.' "

BatTalk
Actor Roger C. Carmel

"I was so bad that it took Batman and the Green Hornet to get me. I liked playing four different characters, like the crazy Russian stamp dealer, Boris Severoff.

"Adam West is a very nice guy, and he took his celebrity very lightly. The assistant director used to call him out of the dressing room by crying: 'Idol of Millions, we are ready for you on the set.' Adam would then come out of his dressing room and, while saying thank you, would take bows."

Special BatEquipment

Batcomputer Ingester Switch
Dual Identity Batsensor
Well-Known Criminal's File
Batmagnifier
Batfunnel
Empty Alphabet Soup Batcontainer

Trivia Quiz 43

What newspaper does Britt Reid publish?

87—KING TUT'S COUP
88—BATMAN'S WATERLOO

GUEST CAST

King Tut—Victor Buono
Lisa Carson—Lee Meriwether
Neila—Grace Lee Whitney
Royal Jester—Tim O'Kelly
Lord Chancellor—Lloyd Haynes
Deputy Mayor Zorty—Tol Avery
Irish Cop—James O'Hara
Guard—Joseph Abdullah
John E. Carson—Nelson Olmsted
Officer—Walter Reed
Jolly Jackson—Tommy Noonan
Fouad Sphinx—Richard Bakalyan
Penny—Terri Messina
Valet—Barry Dennen
Cameo (Window)—Susie Knickerbocker

Teleplay by Stanley Ralph Ross
Story by Leo & Pauline Townsend
Directed by James B. Clark
Production #9755
Original air dates: 3/8/67 & 3/9/67

PLOT

King Tut's Coup. King Tut, with the help of his Tutlings, makes off with a jeweled sarcophagus from Gotham City museum, alerting Batman that he has returned to claim Gotham City as his own.

While Tut prepares to kidnap Lisa Carson, daughter of wealthy socialite John E. Carson, who will be attending an Egyptian Costume Ball as Cleopatra, Batman races to the home of Egyptian pantomimist Fouad Sphinx, where they discover a message left by King Tut, which warns them of Tut's planned revenge on the duo.

Suspecting Tut will make an appearance at the Ball, Gordon has several police officers stand guard there. When Deputy Mayor Zorty arrives dressed as King Tut, they mis-

take him for the real Tut and arrest him. With the police out of the way, the real Tut arrives and dances off with Lisa in front of everyone.

Tracing Tut to his hideout, the duo are overcome, and Batman is locked inside the stolen sarcophagus and lowered into a vat of water to drown.

Batman's Waterloo. Batman uses the Emergency Wireless Batransmitter to alert Alfred with Morse Batcode to his present location. The faithful butler arrives just in time to rescue Batman from the sunken casket. After Batman revives from the trance he put himself into in order to conserve air, Alfred informs him that he overheard Tut planning to boil Robin in oil.

Meanwhile, Tut decides to accept the money Lisa's father is prepared to pay for her safe return, and, using a radio program as the go-between, arranges for Batman to deliver the money to the abandoned boilerworks, alone.

As Tut prepares to boil the Boy Wonder, his current queen, Neila, tries to help Lisa and Robin escape, but all are quickly captured by Tut. Just as Robin is about to be thrown into the boiling vat of oil, Batman uses the battering ram attached to the Batcycle and bursts into the room. Quickly knocking Tut's men out of the way with a money bag, Batman throws a capsule into the oil, turning it into foam rubber. Saved, Robin aids Batman in defeating the Tutlings. Meanwhile, Tut, knocked out during the fight, reverts to his normal scholarly self.

BatFacts

- Not quite hidden in the background of Tut's hideout is a cardboard box with a question mark on it. It was obviously left over from the last Riddler episode.
- Victor Buono died on January 2, 1982, at the age of forty-three.
- The name "Lisa Carson" was the real name of writer Ross's wife.

BatTalk

Actress Lee Meriwether

"Victor was wonderful. Victor said to me one day on the set that he knew he was not going to live past thirty-two. That was the one thing I remember about our conversations—well, that and Shakespeare.

"He was so talented; he was very gifted. But I don't think he ever really thought that anyone would ever believe the talent that he knew he had. He was having a lot of fun on the show."

Special BatEquipment

Electronic Translator
Batmobile Tracking Map
Wireless Battransmitter (for emergencies only)
Morse Batcode
Battering Ram

Trivia Quiz 44

What was the exact amount of the queen's ransom Tut asked for in return for releasing Lisa Carson?

117

89—Black Widow Strikes Again
90—Caught in the Spider's Den

GUEST CAST

Black Widow—Miss Tallulah Bankhead
Tarantula—Don "Red" Barry
Daddy Longlegs—Michael Lane
Trap Door—Al Ferrara
Irving Leghorn—Pitt Herbert
Irving Cash—Grady Sutton
Grandma—Meg Wylie
Grandpa—George Chandler
Teller—Walker Edmiston
Irving Bracken—Milton Stark
Irving Irving—Don Briggs
Motorcycle Cop (Officer Goldberg)—Richard
  Krisher
Cameo (in bank)—George Raft

Teleplay & story by Robert Mintz
Directed by Oscar Rudolph
Production #9753
Original air dates: 3/15/67 & 3/16/67

PLOT

Black Widow Strikes Again. Black Widow arrives in Gotham City to commit a series of bank robberies. After using a brain short-circuiter, she simply has to request a large sum of money, and the bank presidents (all named Irving), who have been rendered incapable of independent thought by the device, happily hand it over to her.

While Black Widow and her men count the stolen money in her den, Batman and Robin try to figure out where Black Widow will strike next. Deducing that she is robbing banks alphabetically, they set a trap for her at the Gotham General Bank, where she tries to short-circuit their brains, but, thanks to their Anti-Short-Circuiting Batelectrodes, she fails. She does, however, manage to escape after spraying Batman with paralyzing spider venom.

Using the Odor-Sensitometer Radar Circuit in the Batmobile, they trace Black Widow, via the smell of the gas fumes from her motorcycle, to a small house, where they are greeted by an old couple in a pair of rocking chairs (actually animated dummies). Unable to get an answer from the pair as to Black Widow's location, they return to the Batcave.

After listening to the conversation with the old couple on the Battape Reader, they realize that their voices were amplified and that the couple were fakes. Returning to the house, they locate Black Widow's underground hideout and find themselves caught in a giant spider web, about to be bitten by two giant black widow spiders.

Caught in the Spider's Den. Batman reaches the 5,000-volt mini-charge in his utility belt and, using the web as a conductor, electrocutes the spiders. The duo then proceed to Black Widow's vault, where they find her and her men counting the money from their latest robbery. Spotting them, Black Widow (having reversed the polarity of her brain device) turns Batman's electrodes against him and short-ciruits his brain. Robin, who was not affected by the device (having lost one of his electrodes), is quickly tied up.

Batman, now in Black Widow's power, uses his Remote-Control Batcomputer Oscillator to locate a bank the spidery fiend can rob. The device responds with the answer but also warns that Batman's life will be in danger if he accompanies her to the bank. Black Widow doesn't want to lose the Caped Crusader, so she dresses the male rubber dummy from the front porch in Batman's spare costume and then, disguising herself as Robin, heads off in the Batmobile to rob the bank.

While Black Widow makes off with the money, Robin frees himself, locates the brain short-circuiter, and transforms Batman to his old self. Upon Black Widow's return, they turn the device on her, rendering her helpless.

BatTalk

Writer Robert Mintz

"I was head of postproduction at the time, while that was in production, and I couldn't keep my hands off that show. It was an extremely busy time. This was what I like to call the golden years of 20th Century–Fox Television, because it was at a point at which we were really challenging Universal for the lead in the number of prime-time hours on the air. In 1966 we had about ten and one-half hours of programs on the air, including 'Batman,' 'Green Hornet,' 'Lost in Space,' 'Time Tunnel,' and 'Voyage to the Bottom of the Sea.' I had offices at three studios. I had an office at Fox; an office at Desilu-Culver, which is where Batman was shooting; and I had an office at MGM. I would leave my office when there was a screening of 'Batman,' and I would go over and sit there with [producer] Howie Horwitz. He enjoyed my being there because I made comments. I was supposed to be the overall supervisor of all the shows, but I found myself more involved in 'Batman' to the extent that I came up with this idea of writing one of them. I had written before, and Howie knew me as a writer. He liked the story, he liked the idea, and he had a commitment from Tallulah Bankhead. She had called and said that she wanted to do the show, and he saw this working as a Tallulah Bankhead vehicle. I was so excited about it, and I was working during the day, and then I would get home and write until midnight."

BatFacts

- This was the last performance Tallulah Bankhead ever gave.
- Tallulah Bankhead died on December 12, 1968.

Special BatEquipment

Brain-Wave Batanalyzer,
Batanalyzing Gears
Anti-Short-Circuiting Batelectrodes
Battape Reader
Batoscilloscope Viewer
Remote-Control Batcomputer Oscillator
Odor-Sensitometer Radar Circuit
Utility Belt Mini-Charge
Radio-Frequency Batgenerator

Trivia Quiz 45

What was Black Widow's full name and address?

91—POP GOES THE JOKER
92—FLOP GOES THE JOKER

GUEST CAST

Joker—Cesar Romero
Baby Jane Towser—Diane Ivarson
1st Henchman—Jerry Catron
2nd Henchman—Jack Perkins
Bernie Parks—Reginald Gardiner
Oliver Muzzy—Fritz Feld
Mrs. Putney—Jody Gilbert
Charles—Owen McGiveney
1st Browser—Gail Ommerle
2nd Browser—Milton Stark
Judge—Jan Arvan

Teleplay & story by Stanford Sherman
Directed by George WaGGner
Production #9757
Original air dates: 3/22/67 & 3/23/67

PLOT

Pop Goes the Joker. The Joker appears at Park's Gallery, where he sprays paint all over an exhibit of artist Oliver Muzzy's latest works. Alfred, who happened to be at the gallery looking for a painting for Bruce, alerts the Caped Crusader to the presence of the Joker. Arriving at the gallery, Batman is surprised when Muzzy, who is delighted by the pop art effects of the spray paint, offers the Joker a partnership. Unable to take any action against the Joker, our duo return to the Batcave to await the clown's next move.

Days later, Joker enters and wins an art contest sponsored by rich heiress Baby Jane Towser. He then announces that he has formed an art school for millionaires only. Bruce decides to sign up in order to keep a closer eye on the Joker, who later kidnaps the entire art class and holds them for ransom. Robin, suspecting Bruce is in trouble, rushes to the school, where he and

Bruce battle Joker and his men. They are soon overpowered, and Robin is tied to a giant mobile covered with rotating palette knives, which threaten to cut him to shreds, while Bruce, tied to a chair, watches.

Flop Goes the Joker. As the rotating knives move closer to Robin, Bruce wedges himself and the chair into the mechanical works of the mobile long enough for Robin to work himself loose, remove one of the knives, and disable the controlling mechanism.

Returning to see if the mobile has completed its work, the Joker and his men are attacked by Robin and Bruce. While the duo pin his men to a wall with carefully thrown palette knives, Joker begs Baby Jane to forgive him. Feeling sorry for him, Baby Jane arranges for him to go free. She then takes him back home with her, where, during a chicken dinner, Joker covers her antique table with paint and has his men chop it to pieces. Convincing the gullible girl that he has turned her table into a work of art, she allows him to replace the priceless Renaissance art collection in her father's wing at the museum with the painted remains of the table.

After removing the entire collection, Joker calls Gordon to inform him that, unless he is paid $10,000,000, he will burn the entire collection of paintings.

Unknown to the Joker, Batman replaced the stolen paintings with "childish" paintings created by Alfred. Surprised by the sudden appearance of the Caped Crusaders, Joker manages to escape with Baby Jane, while his men take their lumps.

Planning to get his revenge on Bruce Wayne, and hoping to pick up some loot, Joker heads to Wayne Manor, where, after losing a duel with Alfred, he runs into Bruce's study, where he trips the switch to the

Batpoles. Mistaking it for a secret passage, he slides down one of the poles. Thinking quickly, Alfred activates the Emergency Batpole Elevator, sending the Joker crashing to the top of the shaft. After a couple of trips up and down the poles, Joker surrenders. Later, Alfred has a showing of his "childish" paintings, with the proceeds donated to the Wayne Foundation Free Nursery.

BatFacts

- This episode marked the transition of the Joker from an arch criminal with a superior intelligence into a spoiled brat with a childish mind.
- Actor Fritz Feld (well known to fans of the "Lost in Space" TV series as Mr. Zumdish) is married to actress Virginia Christine—better known as Mrs. Olson in Folger's coffee commercials.

BatTalk

Actor Cesar Romero

"The makeup took about at hour to put on, but the wig was a thing that bothered me more than anything else. The wig was green, of course, but it sometimes photographed red, yellow—everything but green. They would glue the wig to the front of my forehead, and after a while it would give me a headache."

Special BatEquipment

Batradarscope
Emergency Battunnel onto Highway One
Emergency Batpole Elevator
Batnaphtha

Trivia Quiz 46

To what fortune is Baby Jane Towser the heir?

121

93—ICE SPY
94—THE DUO DEFY

GUEST CAST

Mr. Freeze—Eli Wallach
Glacia Glaze (Emma Strunk)—Leslie Parrish
Professor Isaac Isaacson—Elisha Cook, Jr.
Frosty—H. M. Wynant
Captain Carlisle—John Archer
Carol (Woman Skater)—Schutler (Skye) Audrey
Officer #1—Anthony Aiello
Officer #2—Alfred Daniels
Usher—Ron Riley
Coast Guard Officer—Eddie Ness
Cameo (Window)—Carpet King

Teleplay & story by Charles Hoffman
Directed by Oscar Rudolph
Production #9759
Original air dates: 3/29/67 & 3/30/67

PLOT

Ice Spy. Using the ice magnets inside his iceberg hideout to immobilize the S.S. *Gotham Queen,* Mr. Freeze kidnaps Icelandic scientist Professor Isaac Isaacson in order to force him to reveal his formula for instant ice.

Believing Mr. Freeze had an accomplice on board the ship, Batman feeds the passenger list to the Batcomputer, Moments later, it is discovered that ice skating star Glacia Glaze was on board under her given name of Emma Strunk. Convinced that she aided Mr. Freeze, Batman plans to check her out that evening, when he, as Bruce Wayne, will escort Aunt Harriet to the ice show.

Meanwhile, Mr. Freeze has moved to his hideout underneath the Bruce Wayne Ice Arena and uses his pet seal Isolde to deliver his ransom demands for Professor Isaacson, which include a television broadcast by Bruce Wayne at midnight.

That night at the ice show, Bruce and Aunt Harriet interrupt Glacia while she is talking to Mr. Freeze via the radio in her compact. Intrigued by the compact, Harriet opens it and, to her surprise, hears Mr. Freeze. Glacia quickly explains it away as a music box, but Bruce is now positive the girl is working with Mr. Freeze.

Later the same night, Bruce tapes his television message at eleven o'clock, so he can trap Mr. Freeze at midnight when he tries to collect the ransom money.

Meanwhile, Mr. Freeze has been trying to get Professor Isaacson to reveal his secret ice formula by putting him in a quick-freezer. He becomes discouraged, however, when he learns that the intense cold has little effect on the Icelandic professor, who is used to the cold weather.

After injecting the professor with dry ice and returning him to the quick-freezer, Mr.

Freeze is surprised when Batman and Robin appear during Bruce's taped broadcast. Discovering that they have brought phony money, he has his men toss them into the Sub-Zero-Temperature Vaporizing Cabinet, which will instantly vaporize their bodies and make them a part of the ice-skating rink above.

The Duo Defy. Believing the duo have been vaporized, but still fearing discovery, Mr. Freeze returns with his men to his iceberg.

Our heroes wait until Mr. Freeze has departed and then make their appearance from Isolde's sealhouse, after having escaped the cabinet via an emergency exit.

Mr. Freeze, now back in his iceberg hideout (which is hidden among the dozens of real icebergs floating in Gotham Harbor), has been successful in getting the formula from the professor and builds the deadly Ice-Ray Projector, threatening to freeze all of Gotham City. To prove he means business, he freezes selected spots all over the city.

Meanwhile, Batman instructs Gordon to attach the Small Echoing Seal Pulsator to the seal Isolde and release her into Gotham Harbor. Then, tracing the seal back to Mr. Freeze's hideout in the Batcopter, they rescue Professor Isaacson and capture the frozen fiend and his gang before they can escape in his Ice-Sub.

BATTALK

Actor Eli Wallach

"When my kids were little, they'd always plead with me to appear on 'Captain Kangaroo' or 'Batman' or 'Rawhide,' 'Howdy Doody,' . . . Otto Preminger (who created Mr. Freeze) was unavailable for one sequence, so I stepped into that character, with his German accent intact. I saw little of Batman and Robin since I was the heavy, but it was a fun experience for me. For years afterward, I was respected and honored by my kids. Later I did Trader Eli on 'Captain Kangaroo,' but received only half the kudos that I got for Mr. Freeze!"

BATFACT

- Elisha Cook, Jr., is best remembered as Wilmen the Gunsel in the film *The Maltese Falcon.*

SPECIAL BATEQUIPMENT

Reverse Thermal Batlozenge
Ice Batarang
Ice Batrope
Batpontoons
Super-Thermalized Batskivies
Remote Batmobile Control Phase Advancer
Small Echoing Seal Pulsator (Seal Batsignal)
Anti-Eavesdrop Batplug

TRIVIA QUIZ 47

Where does Chief O'Hara keep the seal while it is at police headquarters?

Third
Season

95—Enter Batgirl, Exit Penguin

Guest Cast

Penguin—Burgess Meredith
Batgirl—Yvonne Craig
Drusilla—Elizabeth Harrower
Reverend Hazlitt—Jonathan Troy
Henchman #1—Jon Walter

Teleplay & story by Stanford Sherman
Directed by Oscar Rudolph
Production #1701
Original air date: 9/14/67

Plot

Hoping to gain immunity from the law, the Penguin kidnaps Barbara Gordon, the commissioner's daughter, with the aim of forcing her to marry him. Batman and Robin learn of the forthcoming marriage from the newspaper's society page and try to locate Penguin's hideout. Penguin's henchmen, ordered to return with a minister, interrupt a meeting between Alfred and Reverend Hazlitt. Alfred quickly offers himself as the minister and leaves with the thugs (but not before he activates the Emergency Batcall in his belt buckle.)

Having located Penguin's hideout in the vacant apartment adjacent to Barbara's, Batman and Robin race to the scene, while Alfred is locked up with Barbara. Believing him to be a minister, she swears him to secrecy and then opens the window and walks along the ledge to her apartment. Entering her bedroom, she activates a secret panel and, after donning her costume, returns to Penguin's hideout as Batgirl.

Joining the just arrived duo, Batgirl helps overcome Penguin and his men. Meanwhile, Alfred, who had been listening at the locked door, has deduced that Batgirl is really Barbara Gordon.

As Batman and Robin try to rescue Alfred and Barbara from the locked room, Batgirl makes her exit. However, Penguin has recovered from the battle and knocks the duo out with Penguin gas. Then, after bagging them, along with Alfred and what he thinks is Barbara but is actually a wedding dress stuffed with pillows, he throws them off the terrace to his waiting truck, which takes them to Penguin's alternate hideout. Barbara spots Penguin making his escape in the truck and changes into her Batgirl guise. Batgirl follows the truck to the hideout on her Batgirlcycle and arrives in time to prevent the duo from being dunked in a vat of boiling water like a pair of giant teabags. While the duo battle the Penguin, Batgirl confronts Alfred. He informs her that he chose to take the minister's place to protect him and did not mean to deceive her. Forgiving him, she then makes him promise not to reveal her true identity to anyone. Alfred agrees, and she quickly changes into the wedding dress so Batman will not become suspicious of her identity. After bagging the Penguin and his men, Batman and Robin turn to thank Batgirl for her help, but she is nowhere to be found.

BatTalk

Actress Yvonne Craig

"One of the reasons I think they hired me was because I had been a dancer. Howie Horwitz, who was the owner, and producer Bill Dozier both knew that. When I went into the office to talk to them, they also asked me if I had ever ridden a motorcycle, which indeed I had and owned one at the time. I did all of my stunts, and I also did all of the motorcycle riding. However, we never did any film mixing with rear screen projections. You never really saw me going fast down the street on that thing, as I recall, from a head-on point of view. I always was going somewhere, and they just filmed wherever it was I was going.

"The motorcycle ride out of the secret exit was an interesting episode. It was the first day of shooting, and I knew the special effects man from somewhere else at Warner Brothers. We had worked togther a long time. I had been practicing riding out because I was supposed to ride through a brick wall. It was set up like a long tunnel, and he said, 'Look, if you hit this mark and you at that point absolutely stand on it and give it all you got, it will look like you are riding the wall down. It will be real exciting.' I said, 'Terrific!' So, I did exactly as he said, but a little voice in my head said, keep your hand close to the brakes because, if something goes wrong, you would like to be able to hit the brakes.

"Sure enough, the first shot of the day, I went tearing out, and the wall didn't come down. It was made of plywood and I wouldn't have liked to have gone through it. I hit the brakes, and I went skidding sideways, missing the wall by about an inch. Nobody on the other side knew what was going on. They figured somewhere along the line I had chickened out and decided not to do it at all. Anyway, it worked the second time around."

BatFacts

- Aunt Harriet makes the first of two cameo appearances in this episode.
- Dick Grayson gets his driver's license in this episode and is now able to drive the Batmobile.
- Producer Howie Horwitz made a fifteen-minute film (which was never aired) of the Batgirl character for ABC in order to convince the network that the addition of the new character would help the ratings. The network liked it and decided to give the series a chance at a third season.

Special BatEquipment

Batradarscope
Battools
Batalert Buzzer

Trivia Quiz 48

What is Barbara Gordon's apartment number?

96—Ring Around the Riddler

Guest Cast

Riddler—Frank Gorshin
Betsey Boldface—Peggy Ann Garner
Siren—Joan Collins
Kayo—Nicholas Georgiade
Cauliflower—Gil Perkins
Kid Gulliver—James Brolin
Cashier—Peggy Olson

Teleplay & story by Charles Hoffman
Directed by Sam Strangis
Production #1707
Original air date: 9/21/67

Plot

The Riddler, hoping to control prize fighting in Gotham City, kidnaps the current champion, Kid Gulliver, and brainwashes him into throwing his upcoming fight.

While Bruce watches Gulliver fight on TV, the Riddler robs the Gotham Square Garden box office, but not before he leaves behind a blinking metal box. Examining the box in Gordon's office, Batman finds it contains a riddle about a long-buried temple in Southwestern Asia.

Later, the Riddler, dressed in a burnoose, appears on Betsey Boldface's TV show in the guise of Mushy Nebuchadnezzer, the supposed boxing champion of Southwestern Asia. Barbara suspects it's Riddler in disguise and follows Betsey to the Riddler's hideout at a little-used gymnasium, where the Siren tries to put Batgirl under her spell. Since the Siren's power works only on men, she fails. So, the Riddler has his men tie up Batgirl in the steam room, but she manages to escape.

Meanwhile, Batman has solved the riddle and accepts the Riddler's challenge to a fight that night at the Garden. As the fight begins, Batman has the advantage over the Prince of Puzzlers, but this quickly changes when he is doused with metal filings by the Riddler and is immobilized when Betsey, who is hiding under the ring, turns on the giant electromagnet.

While the prince of puzzlers beats up on Batman, Barbara, who has been watching from the audience, leaves to change into Batgirl. Returning, she finds Betsey and turns off the magnet. Seeing that Batman has been set free, the Riddler and his men return to their hideout, with our heroes following right behind. The terrific trio then quickly dispose of the Riddler and his gang.

BatTalk

Actor Frank Gorshin (as reported in *The New York Times*, May 1, 1966)

"When I was first approached to play the Riddler, I thought it was a joke. Then, I discovered the show had a good script and agreed to do the role, but only on a show-to-show basis. Now I am in love with the character.

"I developed the Riddler's fiendish laugh at Hollywood parties. I listened to myself laugh and discovered that the funniest jokes brought out the high-pitched giggle I use on the show. With further study I came to realize that it wasn't so much how I laughed as what I laughed at that created a sense of menace."

BatFacts

- After the disappointing portrayal of the Riddler by John Astin, Gorshin was convinced to make this token appearance.
- James Brolin makes his third and final appearance on Batman in this episode.
- The introduction of the character of the Siren in this episode was an attempt to bridge the gap between each episode, now that the show ran just once a week.

Trivia Quiz 49

What did the Riddler drink when he posed as Mushy Nebuchadnezzer?

97—THE WAIL OF THE SIREN

GUEST CAST

Siren (Lorelei Circe)—Joan Collins
Allergro—Mike Mazurki
Andante—Cliff Osmond

Teleplay & story by Stanley Ralph Ross
Directed by George WaGGner
Production #1708
Original air date: 9/28/67

PLOT

The Siren, alias Lorelei Circe, the world-famous chanteuse who can sing in seven octaves, puts Commissioner Gordon under her hypnotic spell and orders him to hide inside the trunk of the Batmobile and, when it returns to the Batcave, to report back to her with Batman's true identity.

When Gordon fails to show up for a meeting at Barbara's apartment, the Dynamic Duo return to the Batcave, unaware that Gordon is hiding in the trunk.

While Alfred dusts the Batcave, Gordon opens the trunk, steps out, and immediately recognizes him as Bruce Wayne's butler. Deducing Batman's identity, he rushes to the phone to call the Siren, but Alfred quickly sprays Gordon with a can of Batsleep.

Meanwhile, Batgirl suspects the Siren is behind her father's disappearance and traces the Siren to her hideout where she hears the Siren call Bruce Wayne and put him under her spell with one of her high notes (two octaves above high C) and then has him meet her at his office at the Wayne Foundation building.

Batgirl rushes to Gordon's office to use the Batphone to call Batman but reaches Robin. She informs Robin of Siren's plans

and later joins him at Bruce's office. Unfortunately, they arrive too late as Bruce has already signed over everything he owns to the Siren, who orders them out of *her* building. Pretending to leave, they follow the Siren and her men to the roof, where she orders Bruce to jump off the building.

The Siren, spotting Robin and Batgirl, orders Bruce to help her men dispose of the heroic pair, but during the fight Bruce accidentally knocks the Siren over the ledge. Robin quickly grabs her hand, promising to help her if she will release Bruce with an antidote note. Having little choice, she signs the note, releasing Bruce, but in doing so loses her own voice forever.

Later, Batman revives the still sleeping Gordon, who, luckily for our heroes, does not remember a thing.

BATTALK

Writer Stanley Ralph Ross

"The producers would say, 'We need a script.' Then I would say, 'Let me come up with an idea for a good character.' I would then come up with the character, and they would say, 'Go write it.' My first drafts were almost always shootable. My second drafts took me less than part of a day to do.

"The network stayed away from us because we were such a smash. If we had been in trouble, there would have been a lot more network intervention, but because it was such a hit, they figured we knew what we were doing. Usually they cast the actor after the script was written. The only time they would have an actor in mind is when we did the sequences when Batman and Robin walked up the side of a building and someone would come out of the window. Then I would write something in particular for whoever it was in the window."

BatFacts

- Although she had had a long career by the time she appeared on "Batman," Joan Collins was still a relative unknown in this country until she starred on the "Dynasty" series.

SPECIAL BatEquipment

Compressed Steam BatLift
Batcomputer Batresistance Signal
Batearplugs
Criminal Sensor Batindicator

TRIVIA QUIZ 50

Where was the Siren's hideout?

98—THE SPORT OF PENGUINS
99—A HORSE
OF ANOTHER COLOR

GUEST CAST

Penguin—Burgess Meredith
Lola Lasagne (Lulu Schultz)—Ethel Merman
Glu Gluten—Horace McMahon
Armband—Lewis Charles
Visor—Joe Brooks
Racing Secretary—Herbert Anderson
Myrtle—Constance Davis
Photographer—Allen Emerson
Radio Announcer—Gary Owens

Teleplay & story by Charles Hoffman
Directed by Sam Strangis
Production #1703
Original air date: 10/5/67 & 10/12/67

PLOT

The Sport of Penguins. Penguin steals Lola Lasagne's priceless parasol at a photo session highlighting Lola and her prize-winning filly, Parasol. Then, while trying to make off with a priceless folio of famous Parasols, Penguin is interrupted by Barbara Gordon. The bird quickly drops the folio and departs, but not before activating the time bomb in his umbrella and leaving it in a nearby umbrella stand. Barbara quickly calls her father, who in turn phones the Dynamic Duo. Our heroes arrive at the library in time to remove the umbrella before it explodes.

Later, the Penguin is visited by Lola Lasagne, alias Lulu Schultz, a fortune hunter, who was divorced by her rich husband, leaving her only the racehorse named Parasol. Lola planned to enter the horse in the Bruce Wayne Handicap in the hopes of winning the prize money, but when she learns that the prize money will be donated to charity, she joins the rascally bird in a scheme to fix the race so that they both come out the winners.

Penguin and Lola head to Glu Gluten's Glue Factory, where they are caught by the terrific trio trying to buy a run-down horse that closely resembles Lola's horse Parasol. Penguin quickly calls for his henchmen, and the fight begins as Lola steals the horse. While his henchmen battle it out with the trio, Penguin rushes outside and brushes paste all over the Batmobile. So, when Batman and Robin attempt to follow him they find themselves glued to the car.

While the crooked bird tries once again to steal the folio of parasols from the library, Lola spray-paints the glue factory horse to look like Parasol.

A Horse of Another Color. Penguin plans to make a bundle for Lola and himself by entering the glue factory horse in the race as Parasol and the real Parasol under the name of Bumbershoot. Thus, everyone will bet on the fake Parasol, while the Penguin gets rich from a bet on the real horse, which will no doubt be considered a long shot. Needing $10,000 to place his bet, Penguin returns to the library to steal the priceless folio.

- Joe Brooks is best known as the near-sighted Vanderbilt on the "F-Troop" series.
- During the actual horse race, a stunt-*man* is disguised as Batgirl and riding Waynebeau.

Unknowingly, Penguin sets off the Emergency Library Prowler Alarm, signaling Barbara Gordon, who quickly calls her father. Commissioner Gordon calls Batman, who rushes to the library to find that the Penguin has secured the folio. The tricky bird gasses everyone with his umbrella and escapes.

Knowing Penguin is short of funds, Batman places an ad in the collector's newspaper for a folio of parasols. Penguin sees the ad and calls the advertiser, Mr. A. L. Fredd, (who is really Alfred in disguise) and sells the folio to him for the needed amount of money.

Later, when Penguin hears that Batman has returned the stolen folio, he blames Barbara Gordon and sends her a toy penguin filled with a deadly gas.

After making his bet, Penguin has all of the horses (except Parasol and Bumbershoot) in the race scratched via some well-placed itching powder. Deducing Penguin's plan and learning that the bird is planning to ride Bumbershoot in the race, Bruce immediately has his own horse, Waynebeau, entered in the handicap, knowing it is sure to win the race.

Alfred knows Bruce would like Batgirl to ride Waynebeau, as Dick is set to ride the fake Parasol. The butler rushes to the library, where he arrives in time to smother the toy penguin before it does any real harm and then tells Barbara about Bruce's plans for the race.

Later, at the racetrack, Batgirl on Waynebeau easily passes the Penguin and wins the race. Realizing something has gone wrong Penguin rushes back to the jockey room to change into his regular clothes before making his escape, and finds that Batman, Robin, and Batgirl have followed him. Calling his henchmen, he battles the trio, but in the end all are captured.

Special BatEquipment

Antipercussionist Asbestos Batflax
Batbomb Shield
Batcorrectional Signal
Library Paste Bat Dissolving Switch

Trivia Quiz 51

What was the name of the jockey that was originally scheduled to ride Parasol?

100—The Unkindest Tut of All

Guest Cast

King Tut—Victor Buono
Osiris—James Gammon
Shirley—Patti Gilbert
Librarian—Cathleen Cordell
TV Announcer—James Ramsey

Teleplay & story by Stanley Ralph Ross
Directed by Sam Strangis
Production #1709
Original air date: 10/19/67

Plot

King Tut, "retired," has set himself up in a tent on 6th and Albert as a public-spirited crime predictor. After three crimes Tut predicts (and masterminds!) occur, Batman and Robin visit Tut to no avail. Later, Tut has his men rob the soccer stadium and allow Batman to capture them, giving him time to plant a homing device in the Batmobile.

Discovering that the Batcave is under Wayne Manor, Tut calls the house and demands to talk to Batman. Bruce denies all, but the unbelieving monarch demands that Bruce prove it by appearing with Batman in public—or else he will tell the world his secret identity.

Later, Bruce programs the Batmobile to drive by itself and, using a dummy Batman and ventriloquism, confronts Tut. Thinking his plot has failed, Tut practically falls to pieces. The felonious pharoah recovers and predicts that there will be a raid to free the Gotham City's arch criminals, luring Gotham's police to the prison. Meanwhile, Tut steals a set of priceless Egyptian scrolls from the library, which will lead him to the statue of a god, rumored to give the possessor control of the entire world.

Barbara, believing the scrolls are in danger, changes into Batgirl and rushes to the library, only to find that Tut has come and gone. Tracking the overstuffed monarch back to his hideout, she is captured when Tut's new queen, Shirley, hits her over the head, knocking her out. Batman follows the trail left by Batgirl at the library, arrives at Tut's hideout, and with the revived Batgirl, captures the entire gang.

BatTALK

Writer Stanley Ralph Ross

"Most of all, I loved writing for Victor Buono. Victor could take an ordinary line and impart three different kinds of meaning to it with his interpretation."

Actor Victor Buono (during an appearance on the "Tonight Show"

"Batman allowed me to do what actors are taught never to do, overact."

Special BatEquipment

Pocket Batsynchronizer
Batoscilliscope Viewer
Batdummy Closet

Trivia Quiz 52

How did King Tut revert to his evil self this time?

101—LOUIE THE LILAC

GUEST CAST

Louie the Lilac—Milton Berle
Lila—Lisa Seagram
Arbutus—Richard Bakalyan
Acacia—Karl Lukas
Dogwood—Jimmy Boyd
Princess Primrose (Thelma Jones)—Schuyler
(Skye) Aubrey

Teleplay & story by Dwight Taylor
Directed by George WaGGner
Production #1710
Original air date: 10/26/67

PLOT

Louie the Lilac, planning to take over the minds of Gotham City's flower children, kidnaps their leader, Princess Primrose, from the park, right under the nose of Barbara Gordon (who knew her as a former classmate named Thelma Jones).

Louie, of course, knew that Barbara would call Batman (which she did), and has arranged a trap for the duo. While Batman and Robin talk with Barbara, Louie plants a card for Lila's Lilac Shop in the Batmobile.

Our heroes find the card, assume it is a clue and proceed to the flower shop, where they are rendered unconscious by poisonous flowers and a well-laced vase. They recover in Louie's hothouse, about to be devoured by giant man-eating lilacs.

Barbara, followed home by Louie's man Arbutus, locks herself in her bedroom, changes into her costume, and chases off the felon. Alfred informs her that the Batmobile has been located near Louie's greenhouse. He gives her the address and she speeds off on her Batgirlcycle.

Meanwhile, Louie takes Primrose, who is under the power of his lilac spray to the flower-in at the park, where she sings Louie's praises. When the spray wears off, she spills the beans, and unlucky Louie drives off in his flowermobile.

Back at the hothouse, Batman has man-

aged to free a foot; he kicks a nearby flowerpot through the window. The cool air that pours in kills the deadly plants instantly. The duo leap from the greenhouse and battle the returning Louie and his men. During the fight, Batgirl sprays Louie with a can of Powdery Mildew spray, changing Louie into a moldy and decayed version of his former self. Swearing never to go to prison, he throws himself into the man-eating lilacs. After rounding up the remaining gang members, Batman and Robin rescue Louie from the greenhouse, where they find the dead plants haven't done him a bit of harm.

BATTALK

Actor Richard Bakalyan

"This was a fun show to do. I mean, everybody wanted to be on it, only because it was an 'in' show to be a part of, like 'The Untouchables' was years ago. We had such fun doing the one on Louie the Lilac, where we stole all of the flowers in Gotham City. . . .

"Milton is such a fun guy. They kept throwing me off the set, because he kept breaking me up. Everytime he went to do a scene in his costume, I would just stand there and laugh. When I stopped laughing, he knew I was going to laugh, so he started to laugh."

TRIVIA QUIZ 53

The Batgirl theme song was used in only two episodes. Besides this episode, in which other episode was the song heard?

135

102—The Ogg and I
103—How to Hatch a Dinosaur

Guest Cast

Egghead—Vincent Price
Olga—Anne Baxter
Omar Orloff—Alfred Dennis
Gilligan—Alan Hale, Jr.
Old Lady—Violet Carlson
Boy Scout—Billy Corcoran
Policeman—James O'Hara
Indian Man—James Lanphier
Technician—Pat Becker
Petula—Mary Benoit
Professor Dactyl—Jon Lormer
Tender—Donald Elson

Teleplay & story by Stanford Sherman
Directed by Oscar Rudolph
Production #1705
Original air date: 11/2/67 & 11/9/67

Plot

The Ogg and I. Disguised as a delivery boy, Egghead kidnaps Commissioner Gordon from his office at police headquarters with the help of Olga and a getaway balloon. Returning with Gordon to his hideout, Egghead issues his ransom demands: a ten-cent tax for every egg eaten in Gotham City. Realizing the only way to locate Egghead and rescue Gordon is by splitting up, Batman and Robin head to the Bessarovian Embassy, while Batgirl teams up with Alfred to comb the city for the smell of Commissioner Gordon's strong aftershave lotion, which they hope to find emanating from Egghead's hideout.

Meanwhile, Batman and Robin have been conferring with Omar Orloff, the Bessarovian ambassador, who believes that Olga will plan to steal the giant Samovar of Genghis Khan, which is being held for safekeeping at the embassy. Agreeing with Orloff's suspicions, the duo hide inside the samovar to wait for Olga.

While Egghead is out collecting his egg tax

(at Gilligan's Restaurant), Olga and her cossacks raid the embassy and make off with the samovar.

Later, at the hideout, the Dynamic Duo leave the samovar and, as they emerge, are quickly gassed by Olga. Recovering, Robin and Commissioner Gordon find themselves being made into borscht by ambassador Orloff, who is also a loyal cossack, while Batman is being considered by Olga as one of her future husbands (as queen she is entitled to six husbands, one of which is scheduled to be Egghead).

Outside the hideout, Batgirl and Alfred locate the smell of Gordon's aftershave and arrive to rescue the duo and Gordon and to make shish kebab of the cossacks. Just as it seems all is lost, Egghead reveals his secret weapon, two chickens who have been fed a diet of onions for weeks. Egghead and Olga pick up a few eggs and toss them at our heroes. The result of the exploding eggs is a cloud of tear gas. As the trio cry, Egghead, Olga, and the cossacks escape.

How to Hatch a Dinosaur. Egghead, Olga, and the cossacks raid the Gotham City Radium Center and make off with two pounds of radium. Later, when Barbara Gordon visits her friend, Professor Dactyl, at the museum, Egghead and Olga steal the giant fossilized forty-million-year-old Neosaurus egg right from under their noses.

Barbara alerts her father of the theft of the egg, and he in turn notifies Batman. As the Caped Crusader and Batgirl ponder the problem, Egghead plans to use the stolen radium to hatch the giant egg and release the monster on Gotham City.

Simultaneously, Batman and Batgirl remember the Professor Grimes article on revitalizing fossils and, figuring that Egghead plans to hatch the egg, use their Batgeiger counters to trace the radium to Egghead's hideout. Leaving Robin and Batgirl to enter by the front, Batman sneaks around to the back entrance.

Entering the hideout, Robin and Batgirl are quickly captured and forced to watch as Egghead hatches the egg. Egghead then tries to offer the captured pair to the monster as a snack, but as the monster advances, Egghead, Olga, and the cossacks turn chicken and gladly run into the waiting arms of Chief O'Hara and his men. As Batgirl and Robin prepare to battle the monster, they are surprised to see the monster remove its head and expose the welcome site of Batman's cowl. Batman, knowing that it was impossible to hatch the egg, decided to use Egghead's beliefs against him. Donning a Neosaurus costume, he secretly entered the egg and made it appear that Egghead had really hatched a monster.

BATTALK

Actress Anne Baxter

"The set for Olga was absolutely crazy. The costuming alone was hysterical, like reaching into your old dress-up box as a kid. That red wig—they kept putting nice quiet reds on me, and I said, 'No, no, no. We wanted *red.*'"

Actor Vincent Price

"I was thrilled to be on the Batman series. I really felt that it was one of the most brilliant television series ever done and I still think so. The imagination and the creativeness that went into these shows was extraordinary. They were way ahead of their time."

The Batmobile weighs 5,500 pounds and has a completely handformed steel body. It has a 129-inch wheel base, and its over-all length is 225 inches.

BATFACTS

- The Neosaurus costume was a hand-me-down from "The Questing Beast" episode of *Lost in Space.*
- Alfred used to work for the Earl of Chutney.
- Olga used to be a dishwasher at a Bessarovian restaurant.

TRIVIA QUIZ 54

a. What was the name of Commissioner Gordon's pungent aftershave, and where did it come from?

b. What were the title of Professor Grimes's article and the name of the magazine in which it appeared?

c. What did Chief O'Hara order at Gilligan's restaurant?

104—Surf's Up! Joker's Under!

GUEST CAST

Joker—Cesar Romero
Riptide—Skip Ward
Undine—Sivi Aberg
Wipeout—Ron Burke
Skip Parker—Ronnie Knox
Hot Dog Harrigan—John Mitchum
Girl Surfer—Joyce Lederer
Johnnie Green & His Green Men—Themselves:
   Johnnie Green, Marilyn Campbell, Richard
   Person, Robert Van Holten & John
   Trombatore

Teleplay & story by Charles Hoffman
Directed by Oscar Rudolph
Production #1714
Original air date: 11/16/67

PLOT

While surfing champion Skip Parker is side-lined by a telephone call, Barbara Gordon awaits his return on the beach. Upon picking up the receiver, Parker is quickly gassed by a hidden device and is carried away by the Joker and his men. Barbara spies Skip being loaded into the Jokermobile and calls her father, hoping he will alert Batman.

Meanwhile, the clown prince of crime, who hopes to become the surfing champion of the world, transfers all of Skip's knowl-

HEE GUFFAW!! HEE!

egde and ability to himself via a Surfing Experience & Ability Transferometer & Vigor Reverser.

Batman and Robin trace the Joker to his hideout at the Ten Toes Surfboard Shop, where they are surprised by the waiting Joker and his men, who paralyze them with handfuls of poisonous sea urchin spines. While the Joker and his aide, Undine, leave for Gotham Point and the surfing championship, the Joker's henchmen turn the duo into a pair of human surfboards.

Using their Portable Ultraviolet Batray, the Dynamic Duo explode their foam coffins and rescue Skip, who was locked up in a nearby workbench, as the Joker's men flee. Realizing the only way to defeat the Joker is by beating him in the surfing contest, Batman orders Robin to head back to Wayne Manor, change back into Dick Grayson, and return to the beach to judge the contest.

Reaching the beach, Batman finds the Joker using his newly acquired ability and knowledge to scare off all the contestants. So, Batman grabs his surfboard and heads out into the water to compete against the Joker. After losing the contest and a confrontation with Skip Parker, the Joker, knowing he has been found out, retreats with his men to the Hang Five (a local surfing hangout), where the terrific trio dispatch the entire gang.

BATTALK

Actress Yvonne Craig

"The crew and I got along great; the cast—Burt and Adam—very well, although I understand they had had trouble with both of them before I joined the show. I didn't join the show until the third season. By that time whatever trouble they had had with them about being prima donnas, as far as I could tell, certainly with Burt in particular, had vanished. He knew his lines always, he came prepared, and when he finished shooting he went to his dressing room and played chess with somebody. Other than that, he was delightful. All of them were."

BATFACTS

• The surfing footage was borrowed from the film *The Endless Summer.*

SPECIAL BATEQUIPMENT

Portable Ultraviolet Batray
Shark-Repellent Batspray

TRIVIA QUIZ 55

Whose birthday is celebrated in this episode?

105—THE LONDINIUM LARCENIES
106—THE FOGGIEST NOTION
107—THE BLOODY TOWER

GUEST CAST

Lord Marmaduke Ffogg—Rudy Vallee
Lady Penelope Peasoup—Glynis Johns
Lady Prudence—Lyn Peters
Superintendent Watson—Maurice Dallimore
Scudder—Harvey Jason
Basil—Monty Landis
Digby—Larry Anthony
Daisy—Aleta Rotell
Sheila (Duchess)—Nannette Turner
Rosamond—Stacy Maxwell
Kit—Lynley Laurence
The Bobby—Gil Stuart

Teleplay by Elkan Allan & Charles Hoffman
Story by Elkan Allan
Directed by Oscar Rudolph
Production #1711
Original air date: 11/23/67, 11/30/67, 12/7/67

PLOT

The Londinium Larcenies. Batman and Robin, along with Batgirl, arrive in Londinium to solve a series of baffling robberies in which the thieves managed their escape with the help of a man-made fog.

Batman, Robin, and Barbara Gordon pay a visit to Lord Ffogg's estate, because Batman is interested in comparing Lord Ffogg's aftergrass with that of Wayne Manor. While at the estate, Robin learns from Ffogg's daughter, Lady Prudence, that her father and her aunt, Lady Peasoup, operate a school for lady crooks under the guise of a girl's finishing school. While the Dynamic Duo take a tour of the estate, Barbara calls Alfred and has him meet her at the road leading to the estate, where she changes into the Batgirl costume brought by Alfred.

Later, when Batman and Robin leave the estate, they are attacked by Lord Ffogg's staff members, disguised as highwaymen. Batgirl arrives in time to help them rout the felons, who, unbeknownst to our heroes, have placed a fog bomb inside the Batmobile, which explodes moments after the duo return to their Londinium Batcave.

The Foggiest Notion. Batman quickly dispels the fog bomb with the General Emergency Batextinguisher, then returns to venerable Ireland Yard to warn Commissioner Gordon and Superintendent Watson of their suspicions about Lord Ffogg. While there, they are sent a clue that leads them to a pub called The Three Bells, located in the dock area. Down at the docks they find a ship containing priceless mod materials and patterns from Barnaby Street, due to set sail that day. As Robin is underage, he is left outside to guard the ship, while Batman enters the pub, which has been taken over by hippies and mod people and captured by Lord Ffogg and his men.

Outside the pub, Robin has spotted Lady Peasoup and her girls sneaking up on the ship, so he cuts the ship free, but in the

process is captured by the girls and spirited off to Ffogg Place.

Back on the road outside Ffogg estate, Batgirl meets with Alfred and, voicing her suspicions, proceeds to investigate the Cricket Pavilion (where Ffogg stores all of the stolen loot). Lady Prudence sees Batgirl enter the Pavilion and releases a cloud of paralyzing gas, immobilizing our heroine.

Believing Lady Peasoup has secured the ship, Ffogg uses a memory eraser on Batman and departs the pub. Alfred, having traced Batman to the pub, finds the Caped Crusader is suffering from amnesia and returns with him to the Batcave, where he restores his memory with the Recollection-Cycle Batrestorer.

While Batgirl is removed to the dungeon, Lord Ffogg has Robin moved to the winch room at Tower Bridge, where he is tied to the winch that opens and closes the bridge. Batman uses the Batcomputer to locate Robin just as the winch starts to raise the bridge. Using his Antimechanical Batray to stop the winch, Batman frees Robin and battles Ffogg and his men. Ffogg, however, manages to escape by creating another man-made mist with his pipe of fog.

The Bloody Tower. Escaping the fog in the winch room, the Dynamic Duo rush to rescue Batgirl, who is still tied up in the dungeon, about to be finished off by Ffogg and Peasoup with some lethal fog pellets.

Robin arrives at the estate but is spotted and is lured by Lady Prudence to Lord Ffogg's hive of African Death Bees. Meanwhile, Ffogg and Peasoup discover that the lethal fog pellets have gone stale, and they rush off to fetch some more, allowing Batman time to sneak into the dungeon, only to be surprised by the returning Ffogg, who pushes him down the stairs, followed by the fresh fog pellets. While Batman and Batgirl are left to perish in the dungeon, Robin, having been bitten by one of the bees, is left to die in the girls' dormitory, as Ffogg and his entire group leave for the Tower of Londinium to steal the crown jewels. Fortunately, Robin took an African Death Bee Antidote Pill and he rushes outside to the Batmobile to find Alfred waiting patiently.

Meanwhile, Batman disperses the lethal fog with Anti-Lethal-Fog Batspray, releases Batgirl, and uses her rope to perform an Indian rope trick to escape through an overhead grating.

Tracing the gang to the tower, the terrific trio arrive in time to prevent the theft of the jewels. Fearing capture, Ffogg tries to escape using his fog pipe, but Batman thwarts him with a Pipe of Fog Batreverser and arrests the entire group.

BatFacts

- Alfred drove around Londinium in his second cousin Cuthbert's taxicab.
- Aunt Harriet makes the second and final of her two cameo appearances in this episode.

Special BatEquipment

General Emergency Batextinguisher
Recollection-Cycle Batrestorer
Portable Battracker
Antimechanical Batray in the Bat Glove
Compartment
Anti-Lethal-Fog Batspray
 Batfile
African Death Bee Antidote Pill
Pipe of Fog Batreverser

Trivia Quiz 56

How does Batman manage to bring the Batmobile and the Batcomputer to Londinium without revealing his true identity?

108—Catwoman's Dressed to Kill

Guest Cast

Catwoman—Eartha Kitt
Angora—Dirk Evans
Manx—James Griffith
Rudi Gernreich—Himself
Queen Bess—Karen Huston
Woman—Jeanie Moore
Attendant—Gerald Peters

Teleplay & story by Stanley Ralph Ross
Directed by Sam Strangis
Production #1717
Original air date: 12/14/67

Plot

A jealous Catwoman interrupts a luncheon honoring the ten best-dressed women in Gotham City and sets off a hair-raising bomb, ruining the hairdos of all the ladies there. Later, Catwoman invades a magazine fashion show and attempts to make off with all of the one-of-a-kind original dresses. While her henchmen subdue Batman and Robin with some bolts of cloth, Catwoman makes her escape through the models' dressing room. Batgirl arrives to free the duo from the cloth. As men are forbidden to enter the models' dressing room, Batgirl goes in alone, only to be captured by Catwoman. By the time the duo realize Batgirl is in trouble, it is too late—Catwoman has already carried her off.

Catwoman later contacts Batman and informs him of the location of her catlair, where she has tied Batgirl to a giant power pattern-cutting machine, which in a matter of minutes will cut a pattern out of Batgirl. Believing Catwoman plans to steal the Golden Fleece, a solid-gold dress belonging to the visiting Queen Bess of Belgravia, from the Belgravian Embassy, Batman finds himself with a problem. As the catlair and the embassy are miles apart, he has to choose between saving Batgirl and preventing Catwoman from making off with the dress, causing an international incident.

Thinking quickly, Batman phones Alfred and sends him to rescue Batgirl. Alfred disguises himself as the world's oldest hippie in order to prevent Batgirl from recognizing him (tipping her off to the connection between Batman and Bruce Wayne). Having been saved in the nick of time, Batgirl rushes to the embassy to join the Caped Crusaders.

Meanwhile, Batman, having arrived at the embassy, confronts Catwoman, who accuses him of abandoning Batgirl in her time of need. Just then, Batgirl arrives and, together with Batman and Robin, battles Catwoman and her men. In the end, justice triumphs, and the villains are led off to jail.

BatTalk
Writer Stanley Ralph Ross

"The reason Eartha Kitt replaced Julie Newmar during the third season was because Julie was doing a movie at the time. I think it was *McKenna's Gold*."

BatFacts

- Designer Rudi Gernreich later went on to design the costumes for the "Space 1999" series.

Trivia Quiz 57

Where was Catwoman's hideout, and what was the street address?

109—THE OGG COUPLE

GUEST CAST

Egghead—Vincent Price
Olga—Anne Baxter
Old Lady—Violet Carlson
Boy Scout—Billy Corcoran
Bank Manager—Donald Elson
Museum Guard—Ed Long
Passerby—Penelope Gillette

Teleplay & story by Stanford Sherman
Directed by Oscar Rudolph
Production #1705
Original air date: 12/21/67

PLOT

Egghead and Olga, Queen of the Bessarovian Cossacks, raid the Gotham City Museum and make off with Egg of Ogg and the Bulbul Scimitar. Gordon immediately calls Batman and Robin for help. While the Dynamic Duo confer with Gordon, Egghead and Olga plan the theft of five-hundred pounds of condensed caviar given to the people of Gotham City by the Czar of Samarkand and currently being stored in the air-conditioned vault at the Gotham City Bank.

Batman, predicting the villains' next move, races to the bank. While Olga and her cossacks make off with the caviar on horseback, Egghead, newly arrived on his burro, is captured by the bank guard. Batgirl quickly appears and convinces Egghead to rat on his friends, then rides off with him in search of Olga's hideout. Moments after Batgirl and Egghead ride off, Batman and Robin arrive at the bank and, after picking up their trail, take off after them.

Arriving at the hideout, Batgirl finds that Egghead has led her into a trap. She is quickly captured and forced to do a saber dance while the cossacks prod her with iced scimitars. Spotting the Batgirlcycle, the duo battle the villains until Egghead throws the bound Batgirl into a vat of caviar to drown. While the duo rush to her aid, Egghead, Olga, and her men escape, only to wind up in the arms of the police.

BATTALK

Actress Anne Baxter

"Working with Vincent was a delight, and Vincent had a lot of fun with Egghead. He hated the makeup, though; it took forever, and it was very hot.

"I had a Russian friend, and I was supposed to swear at my platoon of cossacks, so I said, 'How do I say, "Stand still" and military things?' I wrote them down phonetically, and when I rattled them off, they came to me and said, 'They sound like swear words.' I said, 'Wait a minute; I'm doing Russian,' but it sounded like 'S.O.B.' However, she [Olga] does spout Russian."

BATFACTS

- This episode was originally part of the previous two-part Egghead/Olga story, but rather than air another three-parter, the producers split up the episodes.

SPECIAL BATEQUIPMENT

Batgeiger Counter

TRIVIA QUIZ 58

Where was Olga and Egghead's hideout?

110—THE FUNNY FELINE FELONIES
111—THE JOKE'S ON CATWOMAN

GUEST CAST

Joker—Cesar Romero
Catwoman—Eartha Kitt
Giggler—Sandy Kevin
Laugher—Bobby Hall
Lucky Pierre—Pierre Salinger
Warden Crichton—David Lewis
Judge—Rusty Lane
Foreman—Gil Perkins
Karnaby Katz—Ronald Long
Little Louie Groovy—Dick Kallman
Louie Groovy's Agent—Joe E. Ross
Mr. Keeper—Louis Quinn
Mrs. Keeper—Christine Nelson

Teleplay & story by Stanley Ralph Ross
Directed by Oscar Rudolph
Production #1715
Original air date: 12/28/67 & 1/4/68

PLOT

The Funny Feline Felonies. Upon his release from prison, the Joker is picked up by the Catwoman in her KittyCar. They soon arrive at a sleazy hotel across the street from police headquarters, where the Catwoman shows the Joker an old parchment that will lead them to the hidden cache of gunpowder they will use to blow a hole in the Federal Depository and clean the place out. Before departing, they alert Batman by shooting at him from the open window.

Batman traces the gunshots to the hotel room and finds the Joker's prison clothes and a corner of the parchment. Moments later, Batgirl arrives and makes off with the fragmented parchment. Returning to the library as Barbara Gordon, she finds the parchment was purloined from the very same library. Locating a microfilm copy, she discovers that it contained an ancient riddle, which when combined with certain clues will lead to the hidden gunpowder.

Solving the riddle, she returns to her father's office to call Batman and arranges to meet the duo at the home of Little Louie Groovy, who owns the first clue, a nightshirt.

The duo arrive just as Catwoman and Joker attempt to make off with the nightshirt. Joker tricks the duo into shaking hands, and then, after shocking them with his Joker buzzer, he and the Catwoman make off with the shirt. Minutes later, Batgirl arrives and revives them. She informs them that the shirt was only half the clue to the location of the gunpowder, and they head for the home of mod clothier Karnaby Katz, the owner of the second half of the clue, in the form of a crib. They arrive too late, however; the villains have come and gone—or have they? Just outside in the bushes, the Joker, Catwoman, and their men wait in ambush for the unsuspecting trio.

The Joke's on Catwoman. As Batman and Robin drive off in the Batmobile, the Joker and Catwoman leap from the bushes, capture Batgirl, and tie her up with deadly Cat Whiskers, which contract when exposed to body heat. Leaving her to strangle to death on Katz's front lawn, they depart. Batgirl manages to turn on the lawn sprinkler, causing the Cat Whiskers to expand, sparing her from certain death.

Batgirl hurries to Gordon's office and arranges to meet Batman at the Grimalkin Novelty Company. Arriving at the villains' hideout, the trio overhear their entire plan. As the fiends leave for Phoney Island to find the hidden gunpowder, they are unaware our heroes are right behind them.

Later, at Phoney Island, the villains discover the gunpowder is hidden somewhere inside the lighthouse. While searching the house, they're surprised by the trio, who try to arrest them. Trying to escape, the Joker accidentally trips a switch, revealing the

gunpowder. Without thinking, the Joker lights a match so he can examine the gunpowder more closely, and as Batman wrestles the match away from him, it is inadvertently thrown into the pile of gunpowder. When the house explodes, Batman quickly protects everyone with Anti-Blast Batpowder. As the trio prepares to escort the gang to jail, Catwoman demands to call her lawyer, Lucky Pierre, who has never lost a case.

Later, in court, Pierre refuses to cross-examine any of the witnesses Batman, who is acting as prosecutor, has called. Unknown to Batman, the entire jury has secretly been replaced with Catwoman's former henchmen, who issue a not-guilty verdict. Unfortunately, the jury foreman loses his disguise at the end of the trial, and Batman recognizes him. Realizing he has been found out, the foreman pulls out a machine gun. Batman quickly disarms him as the Joker and his men rise to battle our heroes. After a rousing fight, the villains are defeated. Lucky Pierre, having just lost his first case, breaks his lucky wishbone and storms out.

BatTalk

Actor Alan Napier

"Julie Newmar was the best Catwoman, but Earth Kitt was kind of marvelous. She did complain a lot on the set, though."

Actress Yvonne Craig

'The production crew on 'Batman' were sensational; they all liked one another. We worked very well together. They had worked together for a long time and were held together by the production manager, who was Sam Strangis, who later went on to direct a couple of them and produce other shows at Paramount. If you are a regular in a series, everywhere except Universal, where they change crews on you, you get the same crew every week, so they all get along and work well together and are pulling for the show."

BatFacts

- This was originally a two-part episode, which was split into two single-part episodes as the producers did not want a cliff-hanger ending suspended over a week's time. The trap that the Dynamic Duo were supposed to be placed in was cut from the story, yet later in the episode the Joker is surprised when Batman, Robin, and Batgirl appear at the lighthouse. He believed they were all dead. When it was decided to cut out the trap, no one apparently caught the error in the Joker's dialogue.

Special BatEquipment

Batdolly
Anti-Blast Batpowder

Trivia Quiz 59

There is a photograph of a president in the courtroom. Which president is it?

112—Louie's Lethal Lilac Time

Guest Cast

Louie the Lilac—Milton Berle
Sassafras—Ronald Knight
Saffron—John Dennis
Lotus—Nobu McCarthy
Gus (Janitor)—Percy Helton

Teleplay & story by Charles Hoffman
Directed by Sam Strangis
Production #1718
Original air date: 1/11/68

Plot

While at Bruce's beach house, Bruce and Dick are kidnapped by two henchmen of Louie, the Lilac, after some ambergris (a whale secretion used to make perfume) is discovered on the beach by Dick. Barbara, who had been at the house during the kidnapping, quickly phones her father, Commissioner Gordon, who calls Batman. As they were the kidnap victims, he finds, of course, they are not at home.

Meanwhile, Bruce and Dick have been transported, along with the ambergris, to Louie's hideout at the Defunct Fragrance Factory on Lavender Lane, where they are tied to some machinery and the ambergris is turned over to Lotus, Louie's perfume expert. Lotus tells Louis that she is going to need scent pouches from several animals. Louie sends his men after the animals and plans for Bruce, being an animal expert, to remove the scent pouches once the animals are secured.

Back in the Batcave, Alfred uses the Bat-computer to locate Bruce and Dick. He alerts Barbara Gordon, who, after dispatching a too-nosey janitor, heads for the factory as Batgirl. The butler also sends the Batmobile to the factory via remote control, in the hope it might be of some use to the captured pair.

Batgirl and the police arrive simultaneously at the factory, and while Commissioner Gordon uses a bullhorn to talk to Louie, Batgirl sneaks inside the factory. She is then captured and placed inside an empty vat, which is about to be filled with the hot oil used to extract the scent from blossoms.

Bruce, who has continually refused to operate on the animals, now offers to do so in return for Batgirl's life. Louie agrees and supplies Bruce and Dick with the two glasses of warm water they request. Then, after locking the pair in the basement with the animals, he goes back on his word and decides to kill Batgirl anyway.

While in the basement, Bruce reveals his latest invention, Instant Unfolding Batcostumes, complete with utility belts, which expand to full size when submerged in warm water. Minutes later, Bruce and Dick, now dressed as Batman and Robin, escape from the basement and meet with the waiting police, who aid them in breaking down the entrance in time to rescue the now out-of-the-vat Batgirl from Louie. The trio round up the entire gang. Then, pretending to rescue the kidnapped millionaire and his ward, the Dynamic Duo enter the basement and return seconds later as Bruce Wayne and Dick Grayson.

BatTalk

Actress Yvonne Craig

"Alan Napier was heaven. He had this darling little dog, and he and I both brought our dogs to the set.

"Neil Hamilton was in his late sixties when he did that [Commissioner Gordon] and always knew his lines. He had been a matinee idol. [Hamilton died on September 24, 1984.]

"Stafford Repp, who played the police chief, got married in the midst of our doing the show."

Special BatEquipment

Batmobile Remote Batcontrol
Instant Unfolding Batcostumes with Utility
  Belts
Bathooks
Laser Bar-Cutter

Trivia Quiz 60

a. Where was Aunt Harriet supposed to be during this episode?

b. What tool did Batgirl use to free herself from the perfume vat?

113—NORA CLAVICLE AND THE LADIES' CRIME CLUB

GUEST CAST

Nora Clavicle—Barbara Rush
Evelina—June Wilkinson
Angelina—Inga Neilson
Mayor Linseed—Byron Keith
Bank Manager—Larry Gelman
Mrs. Millie Linseed—Jean Byron
Telephone Operator—Judy Parker
1st Policewoman—Ginny Gan
2nd Policewoman—Rhae Andrece
3rd Policewoman—Alyce Andrece
4th Policewoman—Elizabeth Baur

Teleplay & story by Stanford Sherman
Directed by Oscar Rudolph
Production #1719
Original air date: 1/18/68

PLOT

Acting on orders from his wife, Mayor Linseed removes Gordon and O'Hara from office and appoints Nora Clavicle, women's rights spokesperson, as the new police commissioner. She, in turn, appoints Mrs. Linseed as police chief. After replacing the entire police force with women, Clavicle instructs her two female assistants to set a trap for Batman, Robin, and Batgirl.

Later, Nora has her two aides rob the Gotham National Bank right under the noses of the policewomen, who are too busy fixing their makeup and exchanging recipes to care about the robbery. Meanwhile, our heroes overhear the police radio report about the robbery and, using the portable Batcomputer, trace the criminals back to their hideout, the Drop Stitch & Company knitting supply warehouse.

As the trio try to capture Nora and her aides, Nora grabs Batgirl and threatens to kill her with a razor-sharp knitting needle. She then admits to them that she plans to destroy Gotham City so she can collect on the insurance policy she took out on it. Nora then orders her aides to tie the trio into a Terrific Siamese Human Knot, which will instantly strangle all of them if anyone moves in the slightest. Leaving them to their fate, Nora and the girls prepare the final step in her plan by uncrating and releasing thousands of mechanical mice loaded with explosives and programmed to explode at sunset.

Meanwhile, Batman has remembered how to escape from the knot and, following his instructions, the three escape the trap. Moving outside, they discover one of the mechanical mice. Batman realizes the danger and rushes off on an errand, while Robin calls Mrs. Linseed in the hopes of getting the police to help. Unfortunately, all of the policewomen are afraid of mice, even mechanical ones, and are of no help.

Moments later, Batman returns with three toy flutes. Selecting a tune that will attract the mice (as they're built around high-frequency radar that will home in on the tune), he instructs Robin and Batgirl to play the flutes and lead all of the mice to the waterfront. Like the Pied Piper, the trio locate every single mouse and lead them to the waterfront to tumble into the water harmlessly. Just then, Gordon, O'Hara, and Alfred, having made a citizen's arrest, arrive with Nora and the girls in custody.

BatFacts

- Elizabeth Baur (4th Policewoman) is the daughter of Fox casting director Jack Baur and would eventually replace Barbara Anderson on the "Ironside" series.
- Larry Gelman is better known as the character of Vinnie on "The Odd Couple" TV series.
- Jean Byron is best remembered as the mother on the old Patty Duke TV show.
- Twins Rhae and Alyce Andrece appeared as lookalike androids in the "Star Trek" episode, "I, Mind," which also featured Batman guest star Roger C. Carmel.

When "Batman" first appeared, stock in National Periodicals, publishers of the Batman comic books, rose ten points in a month.

BatTalk

Actress Yvonne Craig

"I enjoyed doing my own stunts on the show. We would choreograph the stunts on a lunch break or something. When you are doing a show, it can get really dull. You are sitting so long while they set up the lights, then you say a couple of lines, then they tear down the lights again. At least stunts are something that uses your physical energy a great deal."

Special BatEquipment

Portable Batcomputer

Trivia Quiz 61

What happened *only* in this episode?

114—PENGUIN'S CLEAN SWEEP

GUEST CAST

Penguin—Burgess Meredith
Miss Clean—Monique Van Vooren
Dustbag—Charles Dierkop
Pushbroom—Newell Oestreich
Doctor—John Beradino
Mint Supervisor—William Phillips
Thug #1—Abel Fernandez
Thug #2—Angelo Posito
Bank Teller—Richard Jury
Bank Director—John Vivyan
Teenage Boy—David Galligan
Teenage Girl—Pam McMyler
Policeman—Len Felber

Teleplay & story by Stanford Sherman
Directed by Oscar Rudolph
Production #1721
Original air date: 1/25/68

As a promotional gimmick before the first episode, skywriters scripted "BATMAN IS COMING" in the heavens above the Rose Bowl.

PLOT

Penguin and his men visit the U.S. Mint to conduct their own guided tour of the buiding. Later, alerted by the bird's appearance at the Mint, the Dynamic Duo find Penguin outside police headquarters and arrest him. Upon learning that Penguin did not steal a thing from the Mint, they decide to see what he is up to and release him.

Joined by Batgirl, Batman and Robin head to the Mint, where they discover that Penguin has infected the money with the dreaded Lygerian Sleeping Sickness and that a supply of the infected money has already been shipped to the Gotham National Bank.

While Batgirl heads to the bank, Batman and Robin visit Gotham's General Hospital to check on the supply of Vaccine B-6, the only known antidote to the sleeping sickness. Unfortunately, they arrive too late. After giving himself and his men a double dose of the vaccine, Penguin pours the rest of it down the drain, then releases three Lygerian Fruit Flies and leaves the duo to be bitten by the deadly bugs.

Using his All-Purpose Batswatter, Batman disposes of two of the flies. The third fly lands on Robin's nose and is quickly captured with the Battweezers. Before heading back to the Batcave to examine the fly, the duo head to the bank to confer with Batgirl. At the bank, they find that several thousand of the infected dollars have already been distributed to the public.

Not knowing which bills are infected, Batman orders a warning broadcast to the public, urging them to dispose of all their cash. As the people dump their money into the street, Penguin and his gang collect it with giant vacuum cleaners.

While the Penguin sorts his newfound wealth, Bruce calls all of the world's financiers and warns them not to take any of the money now circulating in Gotham City. Unable to spend any of the loot, Penguin threatens to release five-hundred fruit flies in the city unless Bruce instructs the world's financiers to accept his money. After consulting with amateur weatherman Alfred, who informs him that the current weather will be cold and clear, Bruce refuses. Penguin quickly carries out his threat and releases the flies. Believing the flies have carried out their work, Penguin and his gang go out to Gotham City's jewelry stores.

Finding the terrific trio, Gordon, and O'Hara asleep in the street reassures Penguin that his plan worked. But when he stops to remove the chief's gold watch, they all jump up and knock the villains flat. After depositing Penguin in a nearby garbage can, Batman informs the bird that the flies were used to tropical heat and were instantly killed by the cold weather. Incidentally, by giving himself that double dose of vaccine, the Penguin will probably contract the sleeping sickness himself. Upon hearing that news, the Penguin falls fast asleep.

BatTalk

Actor Burgess Meredith (as told to journalist James H. Burns)

"On 'Batman' they ultimately kept a script always ready for me so that when I would be in Los Angeles, they'd have a show all set to go."

BatFacts

- Charles Dierkop went on to costar on the "Police Woman" series.
- John Beradino was doing a parody of his role as a doctor on the "General Hospital" series, whose cast also includes David Lewis, better known as Warden Crichton of the Gotham City State Prison.

Special BatEquipment

Portable Batlab
Insecticide Batbomb
All-Purpose Batswatter
Battweezers
Bat Weather Instruments

Trivia Quiz 62

How much of the contaminated money was distributed by the bank?

115—THE GREAT ESCAPE
116—THE GREAT TRAIN ROBBERY

GUEST CAST

Shame—Cliff Robertson
Calamity Jan—Dina Merrill
Frontier Fanny—Hermione Baddeley
Fred—Barry Dennen
Chief Standing Pat—Victor Lundin
Fortissimo Fra Diavolo—Brian Sullivan
Leonora Sotto Voce—Dorothy Kirsten
Pops the Doorman (Cameo)—Jerry Mathers
Peter (Gun Shop Owner)—Arnold Stang

Teleplay & story by Stanley Ralph Ross
Directed by Oscar Rudolph
Production #1723
Original air date: 2/1/68 & 2/8/68

PLOT

The Great Escape. Shame, the conniving cowboy of crime, escapes from prison with the help of his fianc-e, Calamity Jan, and her mother, Frontier Fanny, in a Sherman tank. At police headquarters, Batman receives a message from Shame announcing that he plans to steal a rock and a roll from the Gotham City Stage. While Batman returns to the Batcave to consult the Batcomputer, Shame, who is hiding out at the Gotham City Central Park Stables, is introduced to the members of his new gang: a giant Indian (Standing Pat), who converses in smoke signals issued by his cigar, and a Mexican with a British accent named Fernando Ricardo Enrique Dominquez (Fred for short).

Back in the Batcave, Batman solves the meaning of the rock and the roll. The rock refers to a diamond, and the roll is really a bankroll, but they are unable to figure out just what is the Gotham City Stage. Meanwhile, Batgirl solves the meaning of the Stage, calls Batman on the red phone in her father's office, and arranges to meet the duo at a downtown street.

Shame and his gang arrive at the Gotham City Opera House, where they steal a diamond pendant and a twenty-thousand-dollar bankroll from singers Leonara Sotto Voce

and Fortissimo Fra Diavolo. Just then, the terrific trio arrive and give Shame and his men a good beating until Jan and Fanny spray them with Fear Gas. As the three cower in fear, Shame grabs Batgirl and departs. At the Batcave, Alfred counteracts the effects of the gas with some Batantidote Powder. While Batman tries to locate Shame's hideout, Standing Pat and Fred return with an acetylene torch and a diamond drill.

While Shame and his gang leave the stable with Batgirl, a horseshoe falls from the doorframe and knocks out Frontier Fanny, who is later captured by the arriving duo. Reviving, Fanny warns them that if anything happens to her, Batgirl is a goner.

The Great Train Robbery. Shame and his gang invade an ammunition shop where, after arming themselves, they plot their next moves. Meanwhile, Jan pleads with Shame to swap Batgirl for her mother, and reluctantly Shame agrees. The next morning he sends Standing Pat to police headquarters to deliver the offer. Accepting, Batman and Robin take Fanny to the Central American Pavilion at the closed Gotham City World's Fair, as requested, where Shame and his gang wait in ambush. When Batman spots the armed villains, he tosses a chemical capsule that makes their metal weapons twenty times heavier than normal. Batgirl frees herself and joins the duo to battle the bare-handed villains. Shame quickly grabs a gun and shoots down a pinata, knocking the trio out long enough for the gang to make their escape.

Later, in Gordon's office, Batgirl relates Shame's plan to commit the Great Train Robbery. Batman quickly remembers a shipment of old money that is being transported by train to the Treasury Department for destruction. Believing this is what Shame is after, the trio rush to the train.

Meanwhile, Shame has used the acetylene torch to sever the train tracks and the diamond drill to break into the money car spraying its occupants with Fear Gas and makes off with the money.

Returning to the Batcave, Batman sends a Batdrone plane to issue a skywritten challenge to Shame. Shame accepts the challenge and agrees to meet Batman alone in the condemned tenement district. Shame double-crosses Batman and secretly has his gang wait in a nearby alley, with orders to shoot when Batman and he are twenty feet apart.

While Shame and Batman slowly walk toward each other, Shame's gang prepares to fire, but they are disarmed by Robin and Batgirl. Shame realizes something has gone awry and pulls a derringer from his hat, but Batman knocks it out of his hand. Shame cowardly begs for mercy at Batman's feet. Pretending to surrender, he knocks Batman over, and the two battle it out in the middle of the street. Batman finally wins, and the gang is led off to jail.

Actress Hermione Baddeley

"I liked Cliff very, very much. I am certain there was something terribly funny that did happen, when we first met, Cliff and I. I know it started us off and we were giggling through the whole thing like absurd children. We really enjoyed ourselves. Cliff was so enchanting and I hadn't seen his beautiful acting and I have loved him as an actor ever since. It was great fun the whole thing and his wife was just enchanting. The Mexican bandit with the British accent was a real funny one. We were sort of laughing at ourselves all the time. You don't always enjoy yourself quite as much as we did in that. I got hit on the head, it might have been the draft going right up and I had the wrong kind of underwear on but I know that Cliff and I were absolutely doubled up, but didn't want to spoil the thing by laughing, so we had to look away and keep away from each other. But I thought Batman was brilliant, he was so nice too. Adam at the time of Batman used to have rather serious talks with me. I don't know how he had the time, but he was very anxious to be a serious actor again."

BATTALK
Actor Cliff Robertson

"I remember that the episodes that I did were the greatest fun—the most fun that I ever had on a show. The director gave me all kinds of latitude to work with the character. When they asked me to do the second show, because they liked the first one so much, I asked them if they would hire my wife, Dina, and they did, casting her as Calamity Jan.

"I recall taking my daughter to see Adam West. She was then five years old and, mind you, I was only starring in movies at the time, which didn't make much of an impression on her. But when she met Adam, she said, 'Daddy, I didn't know you knew such important people.' "

SPECIAL BATEQUIPMENT

Emergency Batcommunicator
Batantidote Powder

TRIVIA QUIZ 63

In this two-part episode, Chief O'Hara refers to a classic old move. What is the name of the film?

117—I'LL BE A MUMMY'S UNCLE

GUEST CAST

King Tut—Victor Buono
Suleiman the Great—Joey Tata
Florence of Arabia—Angela Dorian
Manny the Mesopotamian—Henny Youngman
Rosetta Stone—Kathleen Freeman
Tutling—Tony Epper
H. L. Hunter—Jock Mahoney

Teleplay & story by Stanley Ralph Ross
Directed by Sam Strangis
Production #1725
Original air date: 2/22/68

PLOT

King Tut, who currently is at the Mount Ararat Hospital, undergoing psychiatric therapy with Doctor Denton, escapes during one of their regular sessions when the doctor falls asleep. Tut rejoins his gang, and, after robbing the Rosetta Stone Company of $47,000, they hid out at the Florence of Arabia Bellydancing Nightclub (closed due to a case of stomach flu), run by his current Queen of the Nile, Florence. It is here that he informs his men that he has located a deposit of Nilanium, the hardest metal in the world, right under Wayne Manor. He plans to use the stolen money to purchase an adjacent piece of property from real estate agent Manny the Mesopotamian and then blast a slanting shaft under Wayne Manor.

After consulting with Rosetta Stone and the Batcomputer, Batman uncovers Tut's scheme. He also learns that Tut's shaft is aimed directly at the Batcave and that the Batanium Shield Lining of the Batcave might not survive Tut's blasting. After telling Batgirl to meet them at Tut's mine, our heroes leave through a secret entrance using the Subterranean Blue Grotto Exit, to prevent Tut from spotting the Batmobile.

Meanwhile, Tut's mining foreman, H. L. Hunter, announces that they have struck something too hard to break through with ordinary blasting. Believing they have found the Nilanium, Tut volunteers to do the blasting himself. Just then, the terrific trio appear, ready to arrest the fat pharaoh, but Tut and his gang hop into a nearby mining car and speed off down the tunnel. Wanting to prevent Batgirl from learning what lies at the bottom, Batman has her remain behind to keep watch, as he and Robin run down the tunnel. Unfortunately, Tut has reached the bottom of the shaft and crashed through into the Batcave.

When the duo reach the bottom of the shaft, Tut and his men confront them with the discovery of their true identities. After a short Batfight, Batman uses Batnesia Gas to erase the memory of the Batcave from their minds and then has Alfred deposit them on the front lawn. But the duo discover that Tut escaped up the tunnel during the fight, and they race up the tunnel after him. Just as Tut is about to announce Batman's true identity to the recently arrived Gordon and O'Hara, the roof collapses from the vibration of Tut's loud voice, knocking him unconscious. Coming to, Tut reverts once more to his former scholarly self and remembers nothing that has transpired.

BatFacts

- Tut beats up the Batdummy that was used against him in episode #100. Grabbing it with a sigh of recognition, he joyfully beats it up.
- Jock Mahoney is best remembered as one of the several actors who played Tarzan in the movies.

BatTalk

Actor Joey Tata

"The sets were wonderful. That whole set was fantastic. They had a whole thing on a railroad car. We were in it, and the camera was dollying with us. One of the things they left out because they didn't think it was right, was when we were all toasting each other, and Victor lifts the glass and goes to drink. His beard gets in the glass, and after he finishes he lowers the glass, the beard is dripping down. He went, 'Arrgh!' like a pirate. We thought it was just wonderful, but they cut it out; they didn't like it."

Special BatEquipment

Batcave Subterranean Blue Grotto Exit
Batcompass
Batnesia Gas
Batanium Shield Lining of the Batcave
Bat Directional Finder
Special Batseismological Attachment to the Batcomputer

Trivia Quiz 64

This is the only episode in which King Tut revealed his real name. What is it?

118—THE JOKER'S FLYING SAUCER

GUEST CAST

Joker—Cesar Romero
Verdigris—Richard Bakalyan
Emerald—Corinne Calvert
Shamrock—Jeff Burton
Chartreuse—Tony Gardner
Mayor Linseed—Byron Keith
Professor Greenleaf—Fritz Feld
Mrs. Green—Ellen Corby

Teleplay & story by Charles Hoffman
Directed by Sam Strangis
Production #1720
Original air date: 2/29/68

CHUCKLE!!!
HEE HEE!
TITTER!!!

PLOT

The Joker and his men create a flying saucer scare in Gotham City in order to prepare the people for his latest scheme, to build a flying saucer using the plans he got from a mad scientist cellmate and use it to take over the world.

While the Dynamic Duo visit with Gordon, Verdigris (Joker's henchman, who is dressed as a martian) plants a little green timebomb inside the Batmobile, set to go off at midnight.

Returning to the Batcave, Batman uses the Current Criminal Activity Bat-Disclosure Unit and learns the Joker's plan to build a flying saucer. Knowing the Joker will need a lightweight metal to build the saucer, Batman remembers the supply of beryllium currently stored at the Wayne Foundation Metal Research Wing and sends Alfred to

keep an eye on it. As the duo prepare to join Alfred, the bomb goes off and nearly destroys the Batcave.

Meanwhile, the Joker and his men raid the Wayne Foundation and, mistaking Alfred for a mad scientist, take him back to their hideout and force him to build the flying saucer.

Eight hours later, in the Batcave, the Dynamic Duo have survived the effects of the bomb, thanks to their Anti-Thermal Bat-T-Shirts, and finally revive. They make some quick repairs and try to contact Alfred, who has since completed work on the saucer.

Back at the Joker's hideout at the Abandonded Launching Pad Factory on Flying Circus Hill, Batgirl, having followed the Joker from the Wayne Foundation, has been captured and is about to be launched into orbit by the Joker. She foils the clown's plan with her Automatic Fuse Extinguisher. Having wasted enough time, the Joker has her put aboard the saucer along with Alfred and his gang. Moments later, the saucer takes off and heads for outer space. Alfred finally reaches Batman on a tiny two-way radio concealed in his handkerchief. He informs them that he placed some homing beryllium in the saucer, which will force it to return to the abandoned factory. As the Joker begins his ultimatum from outer space, the saucer automatically returns to the factory, where the waiting duo put the Joker and his men into orbit.

HAA HAA HAA!

BatTalk

Actor Richard Bakalyan

"Originally, an actor named Marc Cavell was supposed to have played the martian. It was fun to do that—Verdigris and the flying saucer—and anytime you work with Cesar is a pleasure. It was not work doing these shows. We just went and played and had a good time."

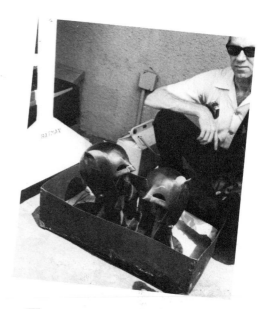

BatFacts

- Although the Joker had a run-in with Alfred at the end of last season's episode, he failed to recognize him in this episide.
- Ellen Corby is well known for portraying Grandma on "The Waltons."

SPECIAL BatEquipment

Current Criminal Activity Bat-Disclosure Unit
Anti-Thermal Bat-T-Shirts
Intercosmic Two-Way Thermophone

Trivia Quiz 65

Stock footage from a classic science fiction film was used to show the Joker's flying saucer in flight. What is the name of this film?

119—THE ENTRANCING DR. CASSANDRA

GUEST CAST

Dr. Cassandra Spellcraft—Ida Lupino
Cabala—Howard Duff
Warden Crichton—David Lewis
Prison Captain—Bill Zuckert
G. David Schine (Floorwalker)—Himself

Teleplay & story by Stanley Ralph Ross
Directed by Sam Strangis
Production #1722
Original air date: 3/7/68

PLOT

Upon learning that the Gotham City Bank has been robbed by two invisible crooks, Commissioner Gordon attempts to call Batman, but is prevented by the invisible Dr. Cassandra and Cabala. After warning Batman that they are helpless to stop them, they depart. While Batman pays a visit to the Gotham City Library where Barbara shows him some books on the occult sciences, Dr. Cassandra and Cabala return to their hideout. There Dr. Cassandra shows Cabala her deadly Alvino-ray gun and warns Gordon that she will now try to steal the famous Mope Diamond from Spiffany's Jewelry Store.

Commissioner Gordon quickly informs Batman and Robin. Joined by Batgirl, they arrive at the jewelry store just as Dr. Cassandra tries to make off with the diamond. Turning her Alvino-ray gun on the trio, she robs them of their dimension. While Cabala collects the flattened heroes, Dr. Cassandra takes the diamond. Later, at police headquarters, Gordon is horrified when the three heroes are slipped under the office door.

Having no one to turn to in their hour of need, O'Hara suggest they call upon the voice that sometime answers the Batphone. Alfred, upon hearing of his employers flattened condition, has them shipped to the

BatTalk

Writer Stanley Ralph Ross

"The producers ran over budget on this episode, and they could not afford to take the two days necessary to block an shoot the fight scenes. So, I wrote this episode in such a way that the fight was in the dark; therefore, the episode was shot in less time.

"Cassandra was named after a little girl who lived next door to me and was always asking to be put into a 'Batman' story."

main post office. Using a disguise, he collects the trio and returns them to the Batcave.

While Alfred figures out how to restore our heroes, Dr. Cassandra and Cabala use their camouflage pills to sneak into Gotham State Penitentiary and release six of Gotham City's arch criminals, returning with them to their hideout in the basement of the Mortar and Pestle building on Abracadabra Lane. They are all issued camouflage pills and given a specific section of the city to rob.

Back in the Batcave, Alfred has put the trio inside the Three-Dimensional Batrestorer and, recalling the Batmobile with the Remote Batcontrol, departs before Batgirl recognizes him. Now fully restored and notified about the breakout at the prison, Batman uses the Special Escaped Arch Criminal Batlocater in the Batcomputer to locate Dr. Cassandra's hideout.

As soon as the trio make their appearance known, Dr. Cassandra and the criminals swallow the pills, making themselves invisible. Unable to see whom they are fighting, Batman quickly turns out the lights, putting them on equal terms with the villains. The trio knock out the entire group, who become visible while they're unconscious. Dr. Cassandra and Cabala are soon on their way to join the arch criminals in jail.

BatFacts

- G. David Schine, the former assistant to the late Senator Joseph McCarthy during the blacklisting trials of the 50s, portrays the jewelry store floorwalker (a.k.a. sales manager) under his given name.

Special BatEquipment

Batrestorer Switch
Three-Dimensional Batrestorer
Anti-Alvino-Ray Batdisintegrator
Batmobile Remote Batcontrol
Special Escaped Arch Criminal Batlocator in the Batcomputer
Portable Batphone

Trivia Quiz 66

Who were the six arch criminals that Dr. Cassandra released from prison?

120—MINERVA, MAYHEM AND MILLIONAIRES

GUEST CAST

Minerva—Zsa Zsa Gabor
Freddy (Touche) the Fence—Jacques Bergerac
Adonis—William Smith
Atlas—Al Ferrara
Aphrodite—Yvonne Arnett
Security Guard—Boyd Santell
Mr. Shubert—George Neise
William Dozier (Cameo)—Himself
Howie Horwitz (Cameo)—Himself

Teleplay & story by Charles Hoffman
Directed by Oscar Rudolph
Production #1726
Original air date: 3/14/68

PLOT

Minerva, the owner and operator of a mineral spa that caters to millionaires, uses her Deepest Secret Extractor to pick the brains of her wealthy customers and to locate their hidden valuables. While Bruce Wayne and another patron discuss the collection of priceless diamonds in the safe at the Wayne Foundation, Minerva eavesdrops and cleverly removes Bruce's wristwatch from the locked box in which he deposited his valuables.

Later, Minerva calls Bruce and informs him that they found his missing watch and that if he comes and gets it she will give him a free Eggplant Jelly Vitamin Scalp Massage. Arriving at the spa, an unsuspecting Bruce is given the full scalp treatment, including Minerva's Deepest Secret Extractor, with which she uncovers the combination to the Wayne Foundation vault. While Bruce leaves, Minerva receives a call from Lord Easystreet, asking her for an appointment. Bruce rushes around the corner to the alley where Robin is waiting in the Batmobile. After changing into his costume he and Robin return to the spa. Suspecting Batman is on to her, Minerva orders her men to put the duo into her Persimmon Pressurizers and parboil them.

While the duo are left to cook, Minerva removes the diamonds from the Wayne Foundation vault and, after rescrambling the combination, hands them over to French Freddy the Fence. Returning to the spa, Minerva finds the duo have escaped— thanks to their Steam-Neutralizing Batpellets—but decides to rob Lord Easystreet before leaving town.

Later, Batman and Robin question Minerva at police headquarters, where she denies knowing anything about their attempted murder or about any of the robberies. Suspecting that Minerva was lying, Batman sets a trap for her, and Barbara agrees

to help by making sure the real Lord Easy-street fails to arrive for his appointment at the spa, (she will notify him that a certain book he is looking for has finally turned up and that he should come to the library right away). While Lord Easystreet heads to the library, Alfred, who is Easystreet's look-alike, takes his place and keeps the appointment at the spa.

Minerva prepares to put Alfred under her Deepest Secret Extractor.

Meanwhile, Batman, upon learning that the combination to the Wayne Foundation vault has been tampered with, uses his Three-Second-Flat Batvault Combination Unscrambler and discovers the theft of the diamonds. Realizing that Alfred is in danger, the duo head for the spa.

Minerva soon learns that Alfred is a fake and tries to discover his true identity. But before she can do so, Batgirl arrives. After capturing Batgirl, she has her men put her and Alfred inside her Persimmon Pressurizers. Then, learning that Freddy the Fence has skipped town with the diamonds, Minerva prepares to leave, but she is interrupted by the arriving duo. Releasing Alfred and Bat-girl, they proceed to battle Minerva's men. As her men keep our heroes busy, she tries to make her escape. Gordon and O'Hara arrive with Freddy, who was captured at the airport, and take Minerva and her now subdued men into custody.

BatTalk

Zsa Zsa Gabor (from the 1984 TV special "Celebrities, Where Are They Now?")

"I loved the character, she was a real wicked woman. The wardrobe was all gaudy and silver and nothing can be more exciting than that. She had a beauty parlor and she had these hair dryers on the people's heads. These hair dryers got all of the spy stories out of the people's brains and I could find out what they were thinking. One person for example was a jewelry salesman and I could find out the combination to his safe. I opened that safe and diamonds kept on falling all over me. I loved it."

BatFacts

- The role of Minerva was originally intended for Mae West, who was at the time preparing to star in the film *Myra Breckinridge.*
- Producers William Dozier and Howie Horwitz, knowing this was going to be the final episode, made "gag" cameo appearances as two of Minerva's millionaire customers.

Special BatEquipment

Steam-Neutralizing Batpellets
Three-Second-Flat Batvault Combination Unscrambler

Trivia Quiz 67

Chief O'Hara suffered an accident in this episode. How did it occur?

161

EPILOG

NBC's unfortunate delay destroyed the series' only remaining chance for a fourth season. How the series would have fared on the new network is unknown. It might have been restored to its original two part/two night format and lasted a few more years, or it might have just gotten worse and died a death of neglect at the end of the fourth year. There are endless possibilities.

However, in September 1969, Batman's 120 episodes exploded into the syndication market where it remains so successfully today, entertaining countless numbers of people in this country and all over the world, more than twenty years after the premiere of its first episode.

In conclusion I would like to recommend that you • • •

tune in next week SAME BATTIME . . . SAME BATCHANNEL!

¿?¡ TRIVIA

1. 2F-3567; TP-6597; BAT-1; 2EF-456
2. House of Ali Baba Jewelry Store
3. "What's My Crime?"
4. Dr. Shivel
5. *The Truth About Bats*
6. Whitey
7. *Male Mode* magazine
8. Pete the Swede
9. a. The BMT
   b. "To the friends of Batman: Many are called, but two are chosen."
10. a. Tinkerbell
    b. 132 pounds, 10 ounces
11. Floyd's of Dublin Insurance Co.
12. Dr. Riddler's Instant Forever Stick Invisible Wax Emulsion
13. Let Gayfellow Take You to the Cleaners
14. a. He was struck on the head during a student riot.
    b. He was supposed to have died in a warehouse fire.
15. a. The Delight of Cooking
    b. The Secret of Success . . . Self-Control
    c. For Whom the Bell Tolls
16. a. An explosive eclair
    b. Aunt Harriet's Birthday
17. Alfred normally orders the caviar through the Iranian Embassy.
18. a. Hecate
    b. Folded Arms Restaurant

c. P. N. Gwynne
d. On the corner of 73rd Street and Concord Avenue
e. It was Peter Lorre's Pet in the 1961 film *Voyage to the Bottom of the Sea.*
f. The wavelength frequency of the Polaris missle is 164.1.

19. a. Alfred was known as the "William Tell of Liverpool." He is an expert with the long-, short-, and crossbow.
    b. Seventeen arrows for $1.
20. Benedict Arnold and the Traitors
21. A griffin
22. a. Ninety-five thousand gallons
    b. Commissioner Gordon's
23. *The Woman in Red*
24. Bruce's birthday
25. a. Bruce was the junior marble champ of Gotham City at age eleven.
    b. Blankets, souvenirs, tacos, pizza, blintzes
26. 99999-79
27. The 13th floor
28. a. Batman, pineapple; Robin, lime
    b. Miss Iceland, Miss Corsica, Miss Canary Islands, Miss Gotham City and Miss Barrier Reef
29. a. "Green Hornet"
    b. Clavier Ankh
30. Alfred portrayed Ethelbert Soames of Soames, Stillwell & Thistlewaite.

QUIZ ANSWERS

31. On the corner of Surf Avenue and 20th Street
32. P-1
33. Hugh Downs
34. Secret writing
35. Nap resembles Stan Laurel, and Snooze resembles Oliver Hardy.
36. Alfred's cousin Egbert's wife, Maudie, is the cleaning woman who discovered the Batskeletons.
37. It looks like strawberry jelly, but it tastes like strawberry axle grease.
38. Batman talks with President Johnson. Before hanging up the phone, Batman asks the president to give his best to Hubert.
39. Mortimer
40. The Riddler's derby
41. Chief O'Hara and the Anti-Lunatic Squad
42. *Robinson Crusoe on Mars*
43. *The Daily Sentinel*
44. $8,300,487.12
45. Mrs. Max Black, widow, 411 Lava Drive
46. The paper clip fortune
47. In a bathtub down the hall from the commissioner's office
48. 8A
49. Camel grass juice
50. The Grotto Arms
51. Wally Bootmaker
52. He was hit by a brick at a love-in.
53. "The Wail of the Siren"
54. a. Wellington #4, From Sumatra
    b. "Revitalizing Fossil Forms by the Use of High-Energy Radioactive Energy Sources"; appeared in *The Southeastern Regional Journal of Applied Radiology.*
    c. A large milk and a hot pastrami.
55. Barbara Gordon's (It began at the end of the previous episode and continued into this one.)
56. He packs them into crates and passes them off as Dick Grayson's desk and books.
57. In abandoned loft in the garment district on 32 Pussyfoot Road.
58. In an icehouse
59. President Nixon
60. a. Aunt Harriet was supposed to be in shock, upstairs.
    b. A Batgirl Batopener
61. There was no Batfight.
62. $13,000
63. *Low Midnight*
64. Professor William Omaha Mackelroy
65. *Invaders From Mars*
66. Penguin, Joker, Catwoman, Riddler, King Tut, and Egghead
67. He hurt himself playing Ping-Pong.

WORDS

The following is a complete list of every Batfight word that appeared on the screen (including the feature film version).

AIEEE!

AIIEEE!
ARRGH!
AWK!
AWKKKKKK!
BAM!
BANG!
BANG-ETH!
BIFF!
BLOOP!
BLURP!
BOFF!
BONK!
CLANK!
CLANK-EST!
CLASH!
CLUNK!
CLUNK-ETH!
CRAAACK!!
CRASH!
CRRAACK!
CRUNCH!
CRUNCH-ETH!
EEE-YOW!
FLRBBBBB!
GLIPP!
GLURPP!
KAPOW!
KAYO!
KER-SPLOOSH!

KERPLOP!

KLONK!
KLUNK!
KRUNCH!
OOOFF!
OOOOFF!
OUCH!
OUCH-ETH!
OWWW!
OW-ETH!
PAM!
PLOP!
POW!
POWIE!
QUNCKKK!
RAKKK!
RIP!
SLOSH!
SOCK!
SPLATS!
SPLATT!
SPLOOSH!
SWAAP!
SWISH!
SWOOSH!
THUNK!
THWACK!
THWACKE!!
THWAPE!!
THWAPP!
TOUCHE!
UGGH!
URKKK!
VRONK!
WHACK!
WHACK-ETH!
WHAM-ETH!
WHAMM!!
WHAMMM!
WHAP!!
Z-ZWAP!
ZAM!
ZAMM!
ZAMMM!
ZAP!
ZAP-ETH!
ZGRUPPP!
ZLONK!
ZLOPP!
ZLOTT!
ZOK!
ZOWIE!
ZWAPP!
ZZWAP!
ZZZZWAP!

ZZZZZWAP!

HOLY

BatWords

HOLY AGILITY
HOLY ALMOST
HOLY ALPS
HOLY ALTEREGO
HOLY ANAGRAMS
HOLY APPARITION
HOLY ARMADILLOS
HOLY ASHTRAY
HOLY ASP
HOLY ASTRINGENT POMITE FRUIT
HOLY ASTRONOMY
HOLY AUDOBON
HOLY BACKFIRE
HOLY BALL AND CHAIN
HOLY BANK BALANCE
HOLY BANKRUPTCY
HOLY BANKS
HOLY BARGAIN BASEMENT
HOLY BAT-TRAP
HOLY BENEDICT ARNOLD
HOLY BIJOU
HOLY BIKINI
HOLY BLACKBEARD
HOLY BLACKOUT
HOLY BLANK CARTRIDGE
HOLY BLUEBEARD
HOLY BOUNCING BOILERPLATE
HOLY BOWLER
HOLY BULLSEYE (2)

The numbers in parentheses after a
specific word refers to the number of
times it was used on the series.

HOLY BUNSONS
HOLY CAFFEINE
HOLY CAMAFLAGE (2)
HOLY CAPTAIN NEMO
HOLY CARUSO
HOLY CATASTROPHE (2)
HOLY CHICKEN COOP
HOLY CHILIBLAINS
HOLY CHOCOLATE ECLAIR
HOLY CHUTZPAH
HOLY CINDERELLA
HOLY CINEMASCOPE
HOLY CLICHE
HOLY CLIFFHANGERS
HOLY CLOCKWORK
HOLY CLOCKWORKS
HOLY COFFIN NAILS
HOLY COLD CREEPS
HOLY COMPLICATIONS
HOLY CONSECRATION
HOLY CONTRIBUTING TO THE
    DELINQUENCY OF MINORS
HOLY CORPUSCLES

HOLY COSMOS
HOLY COSTUME PARTY
HOLY CRACK-UP
HOLY CROSSFIRE
HOLY CRUCIAL MOMENT
HOLY CRYING TOWELS
HOLY CRYPTOLOGY
HOLY CRYSTAL BALL
HOLY D'ARTAGNAN
HOLY DAVY JONES
HOLY DEAD END
HOLY DEMOLITION
HOLY DEPOSIT SLIP
HOLY DETINATOR
HOLY DETONATION
HOLY DEVILTRY
HOLY DILEMMA
HOLY DISAPPEARING ACT
HOLY DISASTER AREA
HOLY DISTORTION
HOLY DIVERSIONARY TACTIC
HOLY DIVERSIONARY TACTICS
HOLY EDISON
HOLY EGG SHELLS
HOLY EPICURE
HOLY EPIGRAMS
HOLY ESCAPE HATCH
HOLY EXPLOSION
HOLY FALSEFRONT
HOLY FATE WORSE THAN DEATH
HOLY FELONY
HOLY FINISHING TOUCHES
HOLY FIREWORKS
HOLY FIRING SQUAD
HOLY FISHBOWL
HOLY FLIGHTPLAN
HOLY FLIP FLOP
HOLY FLOODGATES
HOLY FLOOR COVERING
HOLY FLYPAPER
HOLY FOG
HOLY FORK-IN-THE-ROAD
HOLY FOURTH AMENDMENT
HOLY FRANKENSTEIN (2)
HOLY FRATRICIDE
HOLY FROGMAN
HOLY FRUITSALAD
HOLY FUGITIVES
HOLY FUNNY BONE

HOLY GALL
HOLY GAMBLES
HOLY GEMINI
HOLY GEOGRAPHY
HOLY GHOST WRITER
HOLY GIVEAWAYS
HOLY GLUE POT
HOLY GOLDEN GATE
HOLY GRAF ZEPPELIN
HOLY GRAMMAR
HOLY GRAVEYARD
HOLY GREED
HOLY GUACOMOLE
HOLY GUADAL CANAL
HOLY GULLIBILITY
HOLY H'ORDOURVES
HOLY HABERDASHERY
HOLY HAILSTORM
HOLY HAIRDO
HOLY HALLELUJAH
HOLY HAMBURGER
HOLY HAMLET
HOLY HAMSTRINGS
HOLY HANDYWORK
HOLY HAPPENSTANCE
HOLY HARDEST METAL IN THE WORLD
HOLY HAZINESS
HOLY HEADACHE (2)
HOLY HEADLINES
HOLY HEART BREAK (2)
HOLY HEART FAILURE (2)
HOLY HELMETS
HOLY HELPLESSNESS
HOLY HERE WE GO AGAIN
HOLY HIEDELBURG
HOLY HIEROGLYPHICS (3)
HOLY HIGH WIRE
HOLY HIJACK
HOLY HIJACKERS
HOLY HISTORY
HOLY HOAXES
HOLY HOLE-IN-A-DOUGHNUT
HOLY HOLLYWOOD
HOLY HOLOCAUST
HOLY HOMECOMING
HOLY HOMEWORK
HOLY HOMICIDE
HOLY HOODWINK
HOLY HOOFBEATS (2)
HOLY HORSESHOE
HOLY HORSEHOES

HOLY HOSTAGE (2)
HOLY HOT FOOT
HOLY HOT SPOT
HOLY HOUDINI (4)
HOLY HUMAN COLLECTOR'S ITEM
HOLY HUMAN PEARLS
HOLY HUMAN PRESSURE COOKERS

HOLY HOLE-IN-A-DOUGHNUT

HOLY HUMAN SURFBOARDS
HOLY HUNTING HORN
HOLY HURRICANE
HOLY HYDRAULICS
HOLY HYPNOTISM
HOLY HYPODERMIC
HOLY HYPOTHESIS
HOLY HOLY I.T.& T.
HOLY ICE PICKS
HOLY ICE SKATES
HOLY ICEBERG
HOLY IMPOSSIBILITY
HOLY IMPREGNABILITY
HOLY INCANTATION
HOLY INQUISITION
HOLY INTERPLANETARY YARDSTICK
HOLY JACK-IN-THE-BOX (2)
HOLY JAILBREAK
HOLY JAWBREAKER
HOLY JELLY MOLDS
HOLY JETSET
HOLY JIGSAW PUZZLES
HOLY JITTERBUGS
HOLY JOURNEY TO THE CENTER OF THE
    EARTH
HOLY JUMBLE

HOLY KEYHOLE
HOLY KEYRING
HOLY KILOWATTS
HOLY KINDERGARDEN
HOLY KNIT ONE, PURL TWO
HOLY KNOCKOUT DROPS
HOLY KNOWN-UNKNOWN FLYING OBJECTS

HOLY PRICELESS COLLECTION OF ETRUSCAN SNOODS

HOLY KOUFAX
HOLY LEOPARD
HOLY LEVITATION
HOLY LIFT-OFF
HOLY LIVING END
HOLY LODESTONE
HOLY LONG JOHN SILVER
HOLY LOOKING GLASS
HOLY LOVEBIRDS
HOLY LUTHERBURBANK
HOLY MADENSS
HOLY MAGIC LANTERN
HOLY MAGICIAN
HOLY MAINSTPRINGS
HOLY MARATHON
HOLY MASHED POTATOES
HOLY MASQUERADE (2)
HOLY MATADOR
HOLY MECHANICAL ARMY
HOLY MEMORY BANK
HOLY MERLIN THE MAGICIAN
HOLY MERMAID
HOLY MERRY-GO-ROUND
HOLY METRONOME
HOLY MIRACLES
HOLY MISCAST

HOLY MISSING RELATIVES
HOLY MOLARS
HOLY MOLEHILL
HOLY MOVIE MOGULS
HOLY MUCILAGE (2)
HOLY MULTITUDES
HOLY MURDER
HOLY MUSH
HOLY NAIVETE
HOLY NERVE CENTER
HOLY NICK OF TIME (2)
HOLY NIGHTMARE (2)
HOLY NONSEQUITURS
HOLY OLEO
HOLY OLFACTORY
HOLY ONE TRACK BATCOMPUTER MIND
HOLY OVERSIGHT
HOLY OXYGEN
HOLY PADEREVSKY
HOLY PARAFIN
HOLY PERFECT PITCH
HOLY PIANO ROLL
HOLY POLAR FRONT
HOLY POLAR ICESHEETS
HOLY POLARIS
HOLY POPCORN
HOLY POT LUCK
HOLY PRECISION
HOLY PRESSURE COOKER
HOLY PRICELESS COLLECTION OF
    ETRUSCAN SNOODS
HOLY PSEUDONYM
HOLY PURPLE CANNIBALS
HOLY PUZZLES
HOLY RAINBOW (2)
HOLY RATS IN A TRAP
HOLY RAVIOLI
HOLY RAZOR'S EDGE
HOLY RED HERRING
HOLY RED SNAPPER
HOLY REINCARNATION
HOLY RELIEF
HOLY RECOMPENSE
HOLY REMOTE CONTROL ROBOT
HOLY RESHEVSKY
HOLY RETURN FROM OBLIVION
HOLY REVERSE POLARITY
HOLY RICOCHET
HOLY RIP VAN WINKLE (2)
HOLY RISING HEMLINES
HOLY ROAD BLOCKS
HOLY ROBERT LEWIS STEVENSON

HOLY ROCK GARDEN
HOLY ROCKING CHAIR
HOLY RUDDER
HOLY SARCOPHAGUS
HOLY SARDINE
HOLY SCHIZOPHRENIA
HOLY SEDATIVES
HOLY SELF-SERVICE
HOLY SERPENTINE
HOLY SHAMROCKS
HOLY SHOCKS
HOLY SHOW-UPS
HOLY SHOWCASE
HOLY SHRINKAGE
HOLY SKULL TAMPER
HOLY SKY ROCKETS
HOLY SLIPPED DISC
HOLY SMOKE (2)
HOLY SMOKES (2)
HOLY SMOKESTACK
HOLY SNOWBALL
HOLY SONIC BOOMS
HOLY SPECIAL DELIVERY
HOLY SPIDER WEBS
HOLY SPLIT SECONDS
HOLY SQUIRREL CAGE
HOLY STALACTITE
HOLY STAMPEDE
HOLY STANDSTILLS
HOLY STEREO
HOLY STEWPOT
HOLY STOMACHACHE
HOLY STRAIT JACKET
HOLY STRATOSPHERE
HOLY STUFFING
HOLY STUPOR
HOLY SUBORBIT
HOLY SUDDEN INCAPACITATION
HOLY SUNDIAL
HOLY SURPRISE PARTY
HOLY SWITCH-A-ROO
HOLY TAJ MAHAL
HOLY TARTARS
HOLY TAXATION
HOLY TAXIDERMY
HOLY TEE SHOT
HOLY TEN TOES
HOLY TERMINOLOGY
HOLY TINTINNABULATION
HOLY TIP-OFFS
HOLY TITANIC
HOLY TOME

HOLY TOREADOR
HOLY TRAMPOLINE
HOLY TRAVEL AGENT
HOLY TRICKERY
HOLY TRIPLE FEATURE
HOLY TROLLS AND GOBLINS
HOLY TUXEDO
HOLY UNCANNY PHOTOGRAPHIC MENTAL
   PROCESSES
HOLY UNDERSTATEMENT
HOLY UNDERWRITTEN METROPOLIS
HOLY UNLIKELIHOOD
HOLY UNREFILLABLE PRESCRIPTIONS
HOLY VENEZUELA
HOLY VERTEBRA
HOLY VOLTAGE
HOLY WASTE OF ENERGY
HOLY WAYNE MANOR
HOLY WEAPONRY
HOLY WEDDING CAKE
HOLY WERNER VON BRAUN
HOLY WHISKERS
HOLY WIGS
HOLY ZORRO

171